FIGHT ON!

MARY CHURCH TERRELL'S BATTLE FOR INTEGRATION

DENNIS BRINDELL FRADIN & JUDITH BLOOM FRADIN

Clarion Books / New York

*To our fathers, Myron Fradin
and Harold Bloom, with love*

Clarion Books
a Houghton Mifflin Company imprint
215 Park Avenue South, New York, NY 10003
Copyright © 2003 by Dennis Brindell Fradin and Judith Bloom Fradin

The text was set in 12-point Nofret.

www.houghtonmifflinbooks.com

Printed in the U.S.A.

Library of Congress Cataloging-in-Publication Data
Fradin, Dennis B.
Fight on! : Mary Church Terrell's battle for integration /
by Dennis Brindell Fradin and Judith Bloom Fradin.
p. cm.
Summary: Profiles the first black Washington, D.C., Board of Education member, who helped to found the NAACP and organized pickets and boycotts that led to the 1953 Supreme Court decision to integrate D.C. area restaurants.
Includes bibliographical references (p.174).
ISBN 0-618-13349-6
1. Terrell, Mary Church, 1863–1954. 2. African American women civil rights workers–Biography. 3. Civil rights workers–United States–Biography. 4. African Americans–Biography. 5. African Americans–Civil rights–History. 6. African Americans–Segregation–Washington (D.C.)–History–20th century. 7. Washington (D.C.)–Race relations. 8. Washington (D.C.)–Biography. [1. Terrell, Mary Church, 1863–1954. 2. Civil rights workers. 3. African Americans–Biography. 4. Women–Biography.] I. Fradin, Judith Bloom. II. Title.
E185.97.T47 F73 2003
323'.092–dc21
2002151356

VB 10 9 8 7 6 5 4 3

Contents

Mary Church Terrell's Family Tree

Bold print indicates Mary Church Terrell's direct line of descent.

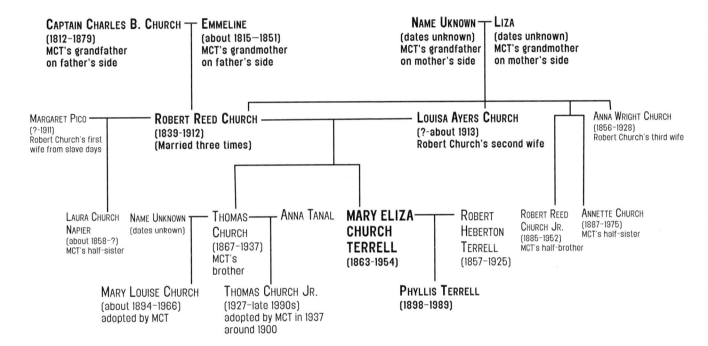

CAPTAIN CHARLES B. CHURCH
(1812–1879)
MCT's grandfather
on father's side

EMMELINE
(about 1815–1851)
MCT's grandmother
on father's side

NAME UKNOWN
(dates unknown)
MCT's grandfather
on mother's side

LIZA
(dates unknown)
MCT's grandmother
on mother's side

MARGARET PICO
(?–1911)
Robert Church's first
wife from slave days

ROBERT REED CHURCH
(1839–1912)
(Married three times)

LOUISA AYERS CHURCH
(?–about 1913)
Robert Church's second wife

ANNA WRIGHT CHURCH
(1856–1928)
Robert Church's third wife

LAURA CHURCH
NAPIER
(about 1858–?)
MCT's half-sister

NAME UNKNOWN
(dates unkown)

THOMAS
CHURCH
(1867–1937)
MCT's
brother

ANNA TANAL

**MARY ELIZA
CHURCH
TERRELL
(1863-1954)**

ROBERT
HEBERTON
TERRELL
(1857–1925)

ROBERT REED
CHURCH JR.
(1885–1952)
MCT's half-brother

ANNETTE CHURCH
(1887–1975)
MCT's half-sister

MARY LOUISE CHURCH
(about 1894–1966)
adopted by MCT

THOMAS CHURCH JR.
(1927–late 1990s)
adopted by MCT in 1937
around 1900

**PHYLLIS TERRELL
(1898–1989)**

Mary Church Terrell.

Who Was Mary Church Terrell?

A handful of people have received the bulk of the credit for the civil rights movement in the United States.

Most people have heard of Frederick Douglass, a great black leader of the 1800s. Dr. Martin Luther King Jr., the leading African American spokesman of the twentieth century, is a household name. Rosa Parks, who refused to give up her seat on a bus in 1955, is remembered for helping to spark the modern fight against segregation. And even people who don't follow sports know about Jackie Robinson, the first black baseball player in the modern-day big leagues.

But there were many other people, largely forgotten today, who played major roles in the struggle for equality for black Americans. Mary Church Terrell, pronounced TARE–ell, was one of them.

Mrs. Terrell was the first African American woman on the Washington, D.C., Board of Education. She was a founder and the first president of the National Association of Colored Women (NACW), an early civil rights organization that opened kindergartens, daycare centers, and night schools for black Americans. In 1909 she helped found the National Association for the Advancement of Colored People (NAACP), to this day a leading civil rights organization.

Mary Church Terrell fought against lynching, worked with Susan B. Anthony to win the vote for women, and laid the groundwork for Black History Month. She was a writer, teacher, public speaker, wife, and mother.

Perhaps the most remarkable aspect of Mary Church Terrell's life is that she did her greatest work when she was nearly ninety. Like many other U.S. cities, Washington, D.C., allowed segregation in restaurants, theaters, and hotels. Starting in 1949, at the age of eighty–six Mrs. Terrell led a campaign to end segregation in the nation's capital. She held protest meetings, picketed restaurants, and organized sit–ins. Her campaign resulted in a series of court trials. Eventually the case was settled by the U.S. Supreme Court, which made a historic ruling shortly before Mrs. Terrell's ninetieth birthday.

Mary Church Terrell's anti–discrimination campaign in the nation's capital helped inspire similar protests in dozens of other cities a few years later. It was also the crowning achievement in the life of a woman who fought for racial equality for more than sixty years.

Dennis Brindell Fradin
Judith Bloom Fradin

Mary Church Terrell in 1953, before a bust of Frederick Douglass.

A Bowl of Soup

One day in January of 1950, eighty-six-year-old Mary Church Terrell phoned three friends to ask them to join her for lunch in Washington, D.C. First she called the eighty-year-old Reverend William Jernagin, a prominent Baptist minister in the nation's capital.

"Reverend Jernagin, will you go to luncheon with me to Thompson's Cafeteria?" asked Mrs. Terrell.

"But we won't be served," said Reverend Jernagin.

"I know we won't be served, but let's go anyway," Mrs. Terrell answered. Chairman of the Coordinating Committee for the Enforcement of the D.C. Anti-Discrimination Laws (CCEAD), Mrs. Terrell explained that the plan was to file suit against the restaurant if it refused to serve them because they were black.

Next Mrs. Terrell phoned Mrs. Geneva Brown, a black woman who was secretary-treasurer of the United Cafeteria and Restaurant Workers Union. Mrs. Brown agreed to accompany Mrs. Terrell and Reverend Jernagin to Thompson's.

A white person should come, too, Mrs. Terrell thought, so her last call was to David Scull, a member of the Religious Society of Friends (also called the Quakers), a faith that had stressed the equality of all people since its founding in the 1600s.

At two forty-five on the afternoon of Friday, January 27, 1950, Mrs. Terrell

Racial segregation was widespread in the United States until about the 1960s; "Colored" referred to black people.

and her three friends entered Thompson's Cafeteria at 725 14th Street N.W. in the nation's capital and joined the food line. Reverend Jernagin went first, followed by Mrs. Brown, Mrs. Terrell, and finally David Scull. Each took a tray and placed a napkin and silverware on it. Reverend Jernagin selected a piece of cake from the food counter. Mrs. Brown helped herself to a salad. Mrs. Terrell took a bowl of soup. David Scull was about to make his selection when a man in a white uniform approached. Identifying himself as the establishment's manager, he said that the three black people could not eat in the cafeteria.

Reverend Jernagin asked why he, Mrs. Brown, and Mrs. Terrell were being turned away. "We don't serve colored people here," the manager replied. "It is against the laws of the District of Columbia and against public policy."

"There is no such law," said Mrs. Brown.

By now the twenty–five people who were eating in the cafeteria had noticed the disturbance and were listening to every word.

"It is management policy not to serve Negroes," said the manager.

"Is this refusal to serve Negroes your rule or a company rule?" asked David Scull.

"It is a matter of company policy not to serve Negroes," the manager repeated.

"The company is refusing to serve me merely because my face is black?" asked Reverend Jernagin.

"Yes, that is why," the manager admitted. "Individually I have nothing against you, but the company will not allow it."

Then Mary Church Terrell spoke up. With her cane and hearing aid, she appeared to be the least threatening of the group, but there was anger in her voice and a determined look in her eyes that made it clear she was a force to be reckoned with. "Do you mean to tell me that you are not going to serve me?" she demanded.

The manager repeated that he couldn't, once again stating that he was not to blame.

"Is Washington in the United States?" Mrs. Terrell asked. "Doesn't the Constitution of the United States apply here?"

After a little more talk, the group left the restaurant without having eaten.

That weekend Terrell, Jernagin, Brown, and Scull visited a notary public— a person who serves as a witness and certifies an individual's signature on a document. They each described what had occurred at Thompson's Cafeteria and had their statements notarized. The following Monday, January 30, Mrs. Terrell and her three friends met with Margaret Haywood, an attorney. Mrs. Haywood accompanied the four to the office of the Washington, D.C., corporation counsel—the city's lawyers. Submitting their notarized statements as evidence, they filed a complaint accusing Thompson's Cafeteria of breaking the law by refusing to serve black people.

Less than a month later, city officials decided that in their opinion Thompson's Cafeteria *had* broken the law by turning away black customers. In order to bring the case to court, however, they asked Mrs. Terrell and her friends to revisit the restaurant and gather more evidence.

On February 28, 1950, Mary Church Terrell returned to Thompson's. Reverend Jernagin was away on a trip to Africa. Mrs. Terrell replaced him with another black minister, Reverend Arthur Elmes, pastor of the People's Congregational Church. Miss Essie Thompson, another member of the United Cafeteria and Restaurant Workers Union, replaced Mrs. Geneva Brown. Once again David Scull was the lone white member of the group.

Mrs. Terrell again selected a bowl of soup while Reverend Elmes and Miss Thompson placed doughnuts and slices of pie on their trays. But the superintendent of the Thompson Restaurants chain of Washington and Baltimore had been warned that the group was coming. He blocked their path to the cash register, saying that Mr. Scull could eat there because he was white but that the other three could not.

Black people in the South were expected to sit in the back of the bus.

Once more Mrs. Terrell and her friends visited the corporation counsel and claimed that they had been victims of discrimination, contrary to Washington law. The city of Washington, D.C., and its attorneys were now ready to bring the case to trial.

The Thompson Restaurant Case, as it came to be known, was to be heard in the police branch of the Municipal Court of the District of Columbia on Friday, March 31, 1950. Mary Church Terrell eagerly awaited the trial. At stake was whether the capital of the United States would continue segregation as usual or begin to topple the barriers that kept African Americans second-class citizens.

This photograph of slaves and slave cabins dates from around 1862.

Bob Church's Daughter

The beginning of Mary Church Terrell's life is cloaked in mystery.

We know that she was born Mary Eliza Church in Memphis, Tennessee, on September 23, 1863, in the midst of the Civil War. We know that her parents were black and had spent much of their lives as slaves. One thing we don't know for certain is whether Mollie, as her family called her, began life as a slave herself.

Tennessee sided with the Confederacy in the Civil War, which was fought partly over slavery. Not until 1865, when the Union won the war, did slavery end throughout Tennessee. It seems possible, therefore, that Mollie began life as a slave. But there's a little more to it than that.

Even in the days of slavery, thousands of free blacks lived in the South. These African Americans either had been freed by their owners or had saved enough money to buy themselves out of slavery.

Mollie's father, Robert Reed Church, had been born a slave on a Mississippi cotton plantation in 1839. He was the son of a slave named Emmeline and her master, a white steamboat captain named Charles B. Church. Captain Church, who was his father as well as his owner, was very fond of Robert. At age twelve Bob was put to work as a dishwasher and servant on his father's riverboats on the Mississippi River. He worked hard and was quickly promoted. By his teens Bob Church was responsible for purchasing the food and drinks for his father's vessels. He

View of Memphis and the Mississippi River around the time of Mollie's birth.

visited hotels, restaurants, and saloons in Memphis and other Mississippi River towns and bought chickens, beef, fruit, vegetables, cakes, and wines. Aboard the steamers he supervised the preparation and serving of food to the passengers.

Somewhere along the line Bob's father may have freed him, but there is no proof of this. Until the Civil War he may have remained a relatively well-treated slave, but a slave nonetheless.

In June of 1862 Northern forces took Memphis and seized boats in the Mississippi River for their use. Bob Church was working on his father's riverboat *Victoria*, which was captured by the Northern fleet. Other crew members of the *Victoria* were taken captive and made prisoners of war, but Bob Church escaped by leaping over the railing and swimming to shore. He made his way to Memphis, where he settled. It is believed that at first he worked in a stable and ran a shoeshine stand. Soon he had saved enough money to buy what would be called the Bob Church Saloon.

That was just the beginning. Church bought more property with the profits from his saloon. He kept buying and quickly became very rich. In late 1862 he married Louisa Ayers, a black hairdresser for Memphis's wealthy white women.

Even though Bob Church was a property owner and a respected Memphis resident, he may still have been a slave when his daughter, Mary, was born in the early fall of 1863. Perhaps the captain didn't harass his son about living like a free man. Or perhaps with the Union in control of Memphis, the captain simply couldn't reclaim his runaway son.

Yet whether her father was a slave or free had little bearing on Mary's situation. Generally, the mother's status determined whether a child was born a slave. If the mother was free at the time that she gave birth, the child was free, too. But if the mother was a slave, the child was born into bondage.

On page one of her autobiography, Mary Church Terrell wrote, "My parents were . . . both slaves." But was Louisa Ayers Church still a slave in September of 1863, when Mary was born? The Union forces that seized Memphis in 1862 liberated most of the city's slaves, so Louisa was probably free at the time of Mary's birth. This means that Mary Eliza Church was probably not born a slave. She was definitely free by the age of two, because the nation's remaining slaves were liberated in 1865.

In her book *Robert Church*, author Cookie Lommel summarized the issue when she wrote: "Mary Church, later Mary Church Terrell, led a very public and very honored life. It did not begin quite so auspiciously, however; like her father, her earliest days may have technically been spent in slavery."

Mary Eliza's life almost didn't begin at all. The first paragraph of her autobiography explains:

> *To tell the truth, I came very near not being on this mundane*
> *sphere at all. In a fit of despondency my dear mother tried to*
> *end her life a few months before I was born. By a miracle she*
> *was saved, and I finally arrived on scheduled time. . . .*

Why and how did Mary's mother try to kill herself? In all of Mary

Church Terrell's 427-page autobiography there is not another word about her mother's attempted suicide, and few details about Louisa at all. As a result, Louisa Ayers Church remains a shadowy and little-known figure to this day. But Mollie wrote a great deal about her illustrious father, Bob Church.

One of Mollie's first memories was traveling by buggy with her father to visit a white man named Captain Charles B. Church on Sunday mornings. Captain Church always welcomed Mollie into his lovely home and gave her fruit and flowers. "You've got a nice little girl here, Bob," he would say, patting Mollie on the head. "You must raise her right."

Mollie adored the elderly white man, but she was curious about something. "Captain Church is certainly good to us, Papa," Mollie remarked one Sunday during their buggy ride home. "And don't you know, Papa, you look just like Captain Church? I reckon you look like him because he likes you."

Mollie, who was four or five at the time, listened as her father explained that Captain Church was his father and her grandfather. He further explained that, although he had been a slave, he had been taught by his father to fight for his rights.

"He taught me to defend myself, and urged me never to be a coward," Mollie's father said.

Mollie had been too young to remember a notorious example of her father standing up for his rights. Following the Civil War, many southern whites were incensed that their former slaves were now free, with the same privileges as themselves. Hate groups, including the Ku Klux Klan (which had been founded in Tennessee), attacked and murdered African Americans. In 1865–1866 about five thousand black Southerners were murdered. Hundreds more were killed in race riots.

In May of 1866, when Mollie was only two and a half years old, a white mob went on a rampage in Memphis, attacking black citizens. Robert Church was warned that he would be shot if he went to his saloon. His wife, Louisa, begged him to stay home, but he wouldn't be intimidated. He was at his saloon when a mob, which included many policemen, burst in. Church was shot in the head and left for dead on the

Mollie Church as an infant, perhaps with her mother.

Mollie's father,
Robert Reed Church.

floor as the thugs drank all his whiskey, smashed the place, and stole five hundred dollars from his money drawer—equal to about ten thousand dollars today. Church survived, but from then on he suffered from excruciating headaches that lasted for days at a time. He was also left with a hole in the back of his head "into which one could easily insert the tip of the little finger," his daughter later explained.

Church's bravery didn't stop there. Forty-six black people had been killed in the Memphis riot, and nearly one hundred black people had been wounded. More than a hundred homes, churches, and schools had been burned. Two whites had also died. When the U.S. Congress decided to investigate, Robert Church agreed to testify.

"In all they shot twelve to fifteen shots at me," he recalled.

"Did you know any of the rioters?" asked the chairman of the congressional committee.

"One of the policemen who shot at me was Dave Roach."

"Do you know where he is now?" the chairman wanted to know.

"He is lounging about the streets yet," answered Church.

"Do you know the names of any of the others?"

"I do not know their names. Most of them were policemen that came into my place. The men that committed the robbery were all policemen."

It took great bravery for Church to accuse the police of attacking him, and incredible courage for him to actually name one of them. Although nothing was done to punish the white rioters, there is no evidence that they took revenge on Church for testifying against them. On the contrary, Church's bravery won the respect of both black and white Memphians, and made him a legendary figure around the city.

Growing up, Mollie saw her father defend himself and his family several times. He earned so much money from his properties that he bought a horse-drawn sleigh. He'd never get to use it in Memphis's warm climate, his friends joked. But one winter there was a heavy snowfall. Robert Church drove up and down Main Street in his fancy sleigh—probably with Louisa, Mollie, and Mollie's little brother, Thomas, who was four years younger than she. Suddenly, a group of ruffians began throwing snowballs packed with stones and rocks at the sleigh. A rock hit Mollie's father in the face, injuring him. Instantly, he pulled out his revolver and fired a shot toward the stone throwers. This was remarkably bold at a time when black Southerners were beaten up and even lynched for such minor offenses as "talking sassy" to whites and refusing to move out of their way on sidewalks. Fortunately, the shot missed. Had he killed or wounded a white person, Church probably would have paid with his life.

Mollie as a little girl.

Mollie and her brother, Thomas, grew up shielded from the difficulties faced by most black people in those days. They lived in a lovely home, traveled in a horse-drawn carriage, and had all the clothes and toys they could want. They didn't know about the lynchings and beatings their people suffered. Nor were they aware that most southern blacks were suffering from practices that became known as "Jim Crow."

Around 1830 a popular entertainer had presented a song-and-dance routine called "Jim Crow," which made fun of black people. "Jim Crow" came to refer to the segregation of blacks from whites by law or custom. After the Civil War, Jim Crow practices forced blacks into separate and inferior accommodations in every aspect of life in the South. Blacks had to ride in separate "Negro cars" in trains, use separate bathrooms and water fountains, attend second-rate schools, and—if they were allowed in at all—sit in the Jim Crow sections of restaurants and theaters.

Mollie's first encounter with Jim Crow occurred when she was five. Her father was traveling to the North on business and took her along. Tennessee's railways were not yet segregated by law, but blacks were expected to ride in separate train cars. Robert Church ignored this custom. He sat with Mollie in the best coach, then left her and walked into the smoking car, perhaps to have a cigar. He had been gone a few minutes when the conductor came by to collect tickets.

Staring angrily at Mollie, the conductor asked, "Who are you and what are you doing in this car?"

The man's attitude confused Mollie. Dressed gorgeously, with two blue ribbons holding her braids, she was "behaving like a little lady" and "sitting straight and proper" just as her mother had instructed before she left on the trip.

A moment later the conductor said he was going to put her where she belonged. He yanked her roughly out of her seat and asked a man sitting nearby, "Whose little nigger is this?"

She was Bob Church's daughter, the man replied, and advised the conductor to let her be. Meanwhile, a white man who knew her father hurried into the smoking car to report what was happening. Church rushed back to his daughter and confronted the conductor. Mary never told exactly what happened, but in her autobiography she hinted that her father had threatened the conductor with his gun. "There ensued a scene which no one who saw it could ever forget," she wrote. "In that section [of the country] at that time it was customary for men to carry revolvers in their pockets," she added.

Back in her seat Mollie asked her father what she had done wrong, but he wouldn't answer and told her not to talk about it. Nonetheless, when she reached home, Mollie asked her mother why the conductor had tried to force her from a nice, clean coach into one that her father said was dirty. She had obeyed her mother's orders, Mollie said. She had kept her hands and face clean, she hadn't mussed her hair, and she had been sitting up properly. Why had the conductor been so cross with her? Her mother patted Mollie's head and explained with tear-filled eyes that sometimes train conductors were mean to good little girls.

Not until later in her childhood did Mollie realize that the conductor had tried to eject her from the car because she was black, and that her mother had cried because she knew that she couldn't protect her children from race prejudice forever. At age five Mollie had no concept of race and simply thought that people came in various colors. Her grandfather, Captain Church, was white, as were many of her friends and neighbors. In fact, until she was six or seven Mollie often called things by their German names because many of her playmates were white children of German ancestry. Mollie and her parents were light brown in color. And her mother's mother—Grandma Liza—was very dark brown.

Mollie first learned about her African heritage from Grandma Liza, who was a wonderful storyteller. Mollie's favorite story was about the "hoop snake." One day, began Grandma Liza, a hoop snake spied a group of children walking through the woods and decided to chase them. Placing his tail in his mouth, the hoop snake rolled toward the children as fast as he could. The oldest child saw the snake approaching and warned the others: "Run, children, run, the hoop snake's after us! Run for your lives!" As Grandma Liza imitated the hoop snake coming closer and the oldest child yelling, "Run, children, run!" Mollie was so scared she could hardly breathe.

But sometimes Grandma Liza told other kinds of stories—true accounts of slaves who had once been owned by cruel masters. One story was about an overseer who had chased Grandma Liza with a whip. Gradually, Mollie realized that her grandmother had actually belonged to another person. Years later she wrote: "It nearly killed me to think that my dear grandmother, whom I loved so devotedly, had once been a slave. I do not know why the thought that my parents had once been slaves did not affect me in the same way."

Seeing how upset Mollie was to hear the true stories about slavery days, her grandmother would comfort her by saying, "Never mind, honey. Grandma ain't a slave no more."

Memphis in the late 1800s.

"Hold High the Banner of My Race"

Her parents hadn't shielded Mollie only from racial hatred. They had also kept their marital problems secret. When Mollie was about six years old, her parents separated. Later they were divorced. At this time Louisa Ayers Church had her own hair salon, known as Lou Church's Store. Mollie and her mother moved into a house a block from Louisa's hair salon. At first Mollie's brother, Thomas, remained with his father, but then a court ordered that he, too, live with Louisa. In those days judges almost always granted custody of a divorced couple's children to the mother.

Although they lived with their mother, Mollie and Thomas still saw their father often. The divorced couple made joint decisions about their children. Mollie's education was a big question. She had attended a school in Memphis that met in a church, but it wasn't very good. Since there were few educational opportunities for black children in the South, her parents decided to send Mollie to school in the North. They chose the Model School, run by Antioch College in Yellow Springs, Ohio.

In the fall of 1871 Mollie's mother took her to Yellow Springs and enrolled her in the Model School. Louisa arranged for Mollie to board with the Hunsters, a black couple who operated an ice cream parlor and the town's only hotel. Louisa Church then returned to Memphis, and eight–year–old Mollie was separated from her family, five hundred miles from home.

Antioch College in Yellow Springs, Ohio, where Mollie attended the Model School.

She adjusted quickly. Mollie liked the school and was welcomed into the Hunster family. Soon she was referring to the couple as "Ma and Pa Hunster." Pa Hunster took Mollie with him in his wagon whenever he visited a neighboring farm to get cream for making ice cream. The Hunsters' four grown children treated Mollie like a little sister. The older son, who walked with crutches, earned his living by running a candy store in the front room of his parents' home. Mollie's father sent her five dollars a month for treats—about one hundred dollars in today's money. She spent much of it at the candy store and the ice cream parlor.

Each morning Mollie walked to the school on the Antioch College campus. One winter day she trudged through a snowstorm to the school grounds. Finding the gate blocked by snow, she climbed the fence, but by the time she reached the top rail, she was so exhausted that she could go no farther. She sat atop the fence for a long time, numb with cold. School must have been canceled, for no one was around to help her. She might have frozen to death if a passerby hadn't noticed her and carried her indoors.

Despite her grandmother's stories, Mollie still hadn't fully realized that she, too, was descended from slaves. She later recalled that it hit her full force one day as her class was reciting a lesson about slavery:

> *It suddenly occurred to me that I, myself, was descended from the very slaves whom the Emancipation Proclamation set free. I was stunned. I felt humiliated and disgraced. When I had read or heard about the Union army and the Rebel forces, I had never thought about my connection with slavery at all. But now I knew I belonged to a group of people who had been brutalized, degraded, and sold like animals. This was a rude and terrible shock. . . . When I recovered my composure I resolved that so far as this descendant of slaves was concerned, she would show those white girls and boys whose forefathers had always been free that she was their equal in every respect. At that time I was the only colored girl in the class, and I felt I must hold high the banner of my race.*

Her opportunities to hold high the banner of her race didn't compare to her father's confrontations with the train conductor or the snowball throwers. Yet to a child who had been protected from race hatred, they were very disturbing.

One day she entered the cloakroom to get her coat and hat and found a group of older girls standing before the mirror, bragging about their looks. "Behold my wonderful hair," said one. "Look at my sparkling eyes," said a second. "And my rosebud mouth," boasted a third.

Imitating the older girls, Mollie said, "Haven't I got a pretty face, too?"

"Your face is pretty—pretty *black*," said one of the young ladies, provoking shouts of laughter.

Mollie was so hurt at being made fun of because of her color that she didn't know what to say. She ran to the door, but just before leaving the cloakroom, she turned around and shouted back, "I don't want my face to be white like yours and look like milk! I want it nice and dark just like it is!"

This experience made Mollie realize that she, too, had shown prejudice. Whenever they had seen a Chinese person, Mollie and her classmates had called out: "Ching, Ching, Chinaman, do you eat rats?" She had never given it a moment's thought. Now she saw that she had been just as cruel as the girls in the cloakroom. Never again would she act with prejudice toward another human being, Mollie vowed to herself. It was a promise she would keep for the better part of a century.

She attended several schools in Yellow Springs for about four years. Mollie was eager to learn and loved most of her classes. One of her few bad experiences came toward the end of a year when the public school she was attending at the time presented a play. Her excitement at being offered a role turned to anger when she discovered that she was to portray a black servant who couldn't speak properly and acted like a fool. Mollie didn't know that a similar routine had inspired the term "Jim Crow," but she was certain that she wanted nothing to do with a play that made fun of her people. She refused to take the part.

It was during her four years in Yellow Springs that she developed a keen interest in reading and writing. Also during that period she had one of the great thrills of her youth. Each month Mollie eagerly awaited her copy of *St. Nicholas*. Among other things, this popular children's magazine featured puzzles and riddles and published the names of readers who solved them. Mollie figured out the solution to a puzzle and mailed in her answer. A few weeks later when *St. Nicholas* arrived, she tore off the wrapping and looked in the back of the magazine. More than sixty years later, she still savored the moment:

> *The first time I saw my name in print I stood speechless with joy as I gazed upon it on a page of* St. Nicholas, *the well-known children's magazine. I must have been nine or ten. . . . There it was—*MARY E. CHURCH—*actually in print. . . . No amount of money could have bought that book from me. It was so precious to me I did not know where to put it for safekeeping. If anybody had tried to take it from me forcibly, I would have fought to retain it till the last ounce of strength had gone.*

A search through old copies of *St. Nicholas* reveals that her name appeared in the back of the October 1874 issue, when she was eleven. It doesn't appear as "Mary E. Church," however. At this time she must have sometimes used her mother's maiden name, for she is listed as "Mary C. Ayers," with the "C" undoubtedly standing for "Church."

In 1875 her parents decided that twelve-year-old Mollie should continue her education in Oberlin, Ohio. Her mother took her to Oberlin and arranged for Mollie to board with a black woman who lived across the street from the high school. Mollie went to eighth grade in Oberlin, then entered Oberlin High. During her four years in Yellow Springs she hadn't seen her parents or brother, Thomas, very often. But after starting school in Oberlin, she spent some holidays with her father in Memphis. Other times she visited her mother and brother in New York City, where Louisa Ayers Church had settled and opened a new hair salon.

Mollie spent the summer of 1876 with her mother and Thomas, recording her experiences in a journal that she saved all her life. In July the three of them traveled to Philadelphia to see the Centennial

---

Can you find Mary C. Ayers, as Mollie called herself, in this list of puzzle solvers at the back of the October 1874 St. Nicholas?

Exposition, a world's fair honoring the hundredth anniversary of the Declaration of Independence. The highlights of the fair included a new invention called the telephone. That summer Mollie also made numerous trips to tourist spots in New York and New Jersey. The twelve-year-old girl described an especially exciting nighttime boat trip in her journal:

A Moonlight Excursion

It was a grand moonlight evening, and everything was as bright as day. Just before the boat made her landing the fireworks began and of course made the boat like some large ball of pink fire. As we went sailing along, everything was on the boat to make it pleasant. Just before we passed Coney Island the bell was rung, and as we looked over we saw that it was all illuminated and fireworks were in progress. . . . We had a delightful trip, for the music and dancing was certainly enough to enliven one. We arrived in New York at one o'clock A.M.

Her mother traveled to Oberlin to see Mollie graduate from high school in June of 1879. Each graduate had to make a speech. In her five-minute talk, which she called "Troubles and Trials," Mollie asserted that most problems were imaginary, and that real ones could be conquered with a positive mental attitude. Mollie practiced what she preached. Her parents had been divorced, she had lived far from home since the age of eight, and she had often been the only black girl in her classes—and through it all she had enjoyed almost every moment of her life.

Following graduation, Mollie went to Memphis to be with her father and Grandma Liza for the summer. Robert Church and his former mother-in-law had remained close and were still friends and neighbors. To make things even better, Mollie's brother also spent that summer in Memphis. Mollie was having a wonderful time with her family when disaster struck the city.

A year earlier, in 1878, Memphis had suffered a terrible epidemic of yellow fever, an often fatal disease spread by mosquitoes. Five thousand of Memphis's twenty thousand people—a quarter of the city's population—had died. In the spring of 1879 several new yellow fever cases broke out in town. But no one was prepared for what occurred that July.

One day a neighbor who had come from Germany rushed into the cottage where Mollie was staying with her father, grandmother, and brother. "Liza, please come see my husband right away," said the woman in broken English. "He's just as sick as he can be."

Grandma Liza, who was known for her nursing skills, hurried to the neighbor's house. Mollie was curious and followed. Entering the room where the sick man lay in bed, fifteen-year-old Mollie saw that his face was yellow.

Mollie's grandmother noticed her and commanded, "Go home *right away!"* Mollie did as her grandmother ordered. When Grandma Liza returned home, she said she was certain the man had yellow fever. She was right. A few hours later he died.

Meanwhile, Mollie's father had rushed in with the news that yellow fever was spreading through Memphis, and that Mollie and Thomas must leave the city because there would probably be another epidemic. Grandma Liza packed their trunks, and that night Mollie and Thomas boarded a train with their father. Robert Church traveled with his children as far as Cincinnati, Ohio. Then, while Mollie and her brother continued on to New York, their father changed trains and returned to Memphis.

Mollie and Thomas spent the rest of the summer in New York with their mother, a thousand miles from the yellow fever epidemic in Memphis. Although it was not as deadly as the previous summer's outbreak, two thousand of the city's people became ill with the disease. Nearly a thousand died. Half the population of Memphis fled to such places as Nashville, Tennessee, and St. Louis, Missouri. Mollie's father and grandmother were among those who remained in Memphis through the epidemic, which lasted four months, until November. Fortunately, Robert Church and his mother-in-law did not come down with yellow fever.

This was an awful period for Memphis. Largely because of the yellow fever epidemics of the 1870s, Memphis went bankrupt. In 1879 its city charter was taken away by the Tennessee legislature. Many people predicted that Memphis was finished and would turn into a ghost town.

At this time, when the future of Memphis seemed so bleak, Robert Church was confident that it would bounce back. He bought up all the land and buildings in Memphis that he could afford. Although the property was cheap, many of his friends thought he was throwing away his money on a dying city. Robert Church did still more. To lead Memphis out of bankruptcy and regain its city charter, Memphis leaders decided to sell municipal bonds. The problem was, people were reluctant to invest their money in a place that seemed to have no future.

Robert Church came to the rescue, buying the first bond for a thousand dollars—about twenty thousand dollars in today's money. Others followed his example and invested in Memphis. In the late 1800s Memphis's population soared, and it regained its city charter. In time Robert Church's investments made him so wealthy that he became known as the South's first black millionaire.

Mollie Church would find that being a rich man's daughter had many advantages—as well as a few drawbacks.

BIRD'S-EYE VIEW OF OBERLIN COLLEGE BUILDINGS FROM COUNCIL HALL.

Oberlin College in the late 1800s.

"I Am a Colored Girl"

Mollie was ill when she arrived in New York City in the summer of 1879. She ran a fever and lay in bed delirious. She may have had a relatively mild case of yellow fever. If so, she never reached the stages of running a very high fever, turning yellowish, and in the worst cases lapsing into a coma followed by death. Mollie recovered completely after several days.

As a high school graduate, Miss Mary Eliza Church already belonged to a select group. She was about to join an even more elite society. In the United States, as of 1880, two thirds of all young white people, but only one third of all black children, were enrolled in school. Few blacks had gone as far as high school. Higher education was so rare among African Americans that between 1875 and 1880 fewer than two hundred black students graduated from college in the entire country.

Her parents had sent Mollie to school in Oberlin, Ohio, in the hope that she would attend Oberlin College. The town and college of Oberlin had been established in the 1830s by people who believed in human equality. Oberlin was the country's first college to grant female students college degrees, and one of the first to admit black students. Before the Civil War the townspeople and the college students had sheltered about three thousand slaves fleeing the South via the Underground Railroad. On one occasion nearly the entire town had taken to the streets to prevent the capture of a runaway slave.

In the fall of 1879 Mollie enrolled in Oberlin College's preparatory department to get herself ready for the rigors of college. She barely passed geometry but excelled in her other classes. The following fall Mollie entered the college as a freshman. The next four years would be among the happiest of her life.

"As a college girl, I was accorded the same treatment at Oberlin College as a white girl," she later wrote in her autobiography. "Prejudice against colored students would not have been tolerated for one minute by those in authority at that time." In Ladies Hall, her dormitory, "never once did I feel that I was being discriminated against on account of my color."

She felt more bias because of her sex than her race. Oberlin offered a choice. Mollie could take the literary course, also called the ladies' course, a simpler two-year program that many female students selected. Or she might take the classical course, known as the gentlemen's course, a more demanding four-year program that male students tended to choose.

Mollie preferred the gentlemen's course. Her friends argued that it would be too difficult, and that it would scare off potential husbands who would consider her too brainy. "Where will you find a colored man who has studied Greek?" one friend asked. But Mollie wrote to her father and explained that, even though it would be more costly, she hoped to take the gentlemen's course. Robert Church had taught himself to read by studying newspapers, but he had never gone to school and couldn't write anything except his name. He dictated a letter assuring Mollie that he would gladly pay for her to study anything she pleased.

Mollie enrolled in the gentlemen's course, taking such subjects as Greek, Latin, French, the Bible, and English literature—often in classes composed mainly of young men. One day the English poet Matthew Arnold visited Mollie's Greek class. While the famous poet looked on, Mollie's professor asked her to read an ancient Greek selection and then translate it into English. Mollie did a fine job, prompting Arnold to admit he had thought black people's tongues were too thick to pronounce ancient Greek properly! If a highly educated poet had such a ridiculous idea, thought Mollie, was it any wonder that so many people had ignorant notions about racial groups they didn't know?

Oberlin freshman Mollie Church.

Hardly an hour of the day passed when Mollie wasn't busy. She sang in school and church choirs. She was an editor of the college paper, the *Oberlin Review.* She joined a literary society and represented it in debating contests with a rival society. Mollie was also elected the class poet.

Besides all this Mollie was active in sports, which wasn't common among young women in the late 1800s. She joined a club that played a new sport called tennis. She went ice-skating in the winter and swam and rode horseback in warmer weather. Mollie also attended all of her school's baseball games, serving as the team's scorekeeper.

During her freshman year Mollie's father sent her a guitar, which she taught herself to play. Sometimes forty or fifty students would go on a picnic to nearby Lake Erie, and Mollie would play her guitar to accompany their singing. But Mollie's favorite pastime was dancing. Oberlin College didn't allow young men and women to dance together. Mollie and another girl in Ladies Hall who loved to dance would go to the gymnasium after supper and try the latest steps together as their friends watched.

In the middle of her freshman year Mollie had a chance to really show off her dancing. One winter morning an invitation postmarked Washington, D.C., arrived for Mollie at Ladies Hall. It came from Senator Blanche Kelso Bruce and his wife. Bruce, a friend of Mollie's father, represented the state of Mississippi from 1875 to 1881. He was the first African American to serve a whole term in the U.S. Senate. The Bruces had invited her to attend the Inaugural Ball for the incoming president, James A. Garfield, to be held on March 4, 1881.

Mollie's mother sent her a beautiful dress from New York, and Oberlin officials allowed her to miss a few days of school. She traveled by train to the

Frederick Douglass.

nation's capital. With Senator and Mrs. Bruce, Mollie attended a succession of dances and receptions, climaxed by the Inaugural Ball. The seventeen-year-old college student met senators, representatives, and judges. She saw the new president, who would die from an assassin's bullet a few months later.

But the highlight of her Washington visit happened by accident. She and a friend were walking down the street when they approached a dignified man in his sixties. Having seen his picture, Mollie knew that he was Frederick Douglass, the former slave who had become the leading spokesman for the rights of African Americans. Her companion introduced Mollie to Douglass, beginning a friendship that would last for the rest of the famous man's life.

Now and again Mary Eliza Church was reminded that she enjoyed a sheltered life at Oberlin. One summer, while living with her mother and brother in New York, Mollie decided to get a job. She found several newspaper advertisements placed by women seeking personal secretaries. Some of her white college friends had obtained similar summer jobs, so Mollie expected to find one, too.

She went to interview after interview but was turned down every time. A woman who seemed on the brink of hiring her said, "I notice you are quite dark," then asked about Mollie's "nationality."

"I am a colored girl," replied Mollie. She herself was not prejudiced, the woman explained, but her white servants might quit if she hired a colored girl. She was sorry, but Mollie couldn't have the job.

Another woman actually hired Mollie and told her to report to work Monday morning. But on Sunday afternoon Mollie received a hand-delivered letter. The woman's daughter had seen Mollie and wanted to know her race. Mollie sent back a note explaining that she was black. That night the messenger returned with a letter saying that the agreement was canceled.

Despite her eagerness to work, Mollie remained unemployed that summer. It was a dose of reality, for if a light-skinned college student from a prominent family was turned down because of her race, what were conditions like for the majority of black people?

In fact, they were terrible. Jim Crow practices were spreading through the South and parts of the North. Blacks suffered daily discrimination in every aspect of life, from housing to the workplace. For example, in 1875 Mollie's native state of Tennessee passed legislation allowing proprietors of such places as hotels and restaurants to exclude black people, and in 1881 Tennessee passed a Jim Crow law requiring black railway passengers to ride in separate train cars from whites.

Meanwhile, Mollie was starting to think about her future. She dreamed of becoming a writer. Because she saved most of what she wrote all her life, the thirteen thousand items in the Mary Church Terrell Papers

A segregated rest stop for black travelers.

A segregated black neighborhood in Memphis.

at the Library of Congress in Washington, D.C., include many of her college writings. During that period she wrote numerous poems, including "The Castle by the Sea" and "The Falling Star," about mysterious castles and magical flying creatures.

She also began to write about social problems. Her essay "Prejudice" discussed various forms of bias, including prejudice against black people. And in her essay "The Poor in Our Cities," Mollie predicted that U.S. cities would one day suffer riots unless something was done to help the poor:

> *That there is poverty in our cities we well know. We all have seen the miserable abodes of the poor, have seen the tale of misery written on their faces, have heard hungry children crying for bread. . . . The poor can be seen on every street. The halfclad children who come with empty baskets to our doors are*

*Mollie Church in 1884,
the year she graduated
from Oberlin.*

always frightful to behold. Poverty everywhere is distressing, and we long to relieve it. . . . The poor must be better provided for, or in time they will rise up against the wealthier class, and the result will be civil war.

Mollie was to graduate from Oberlin on June 25, 1884. In the months before graduation, she later recalled, she realized that "the carefree days of my youth would soon be a thing of the past" and that she would have to "go out into the cold world."

Back in Memphis, Robert Church was determined to keep his daughter as far from that cold world as he could. He sent Mollie a letter stating that after her graduation he would meet her in Louisville, Kentucky. They would spend a few days there before continuing on to Memphis, where Mollie would live with him in his new home.

Robert Church met his daughter in Louisville and stayed there with her for a week and a half. They then took the train to Memphis, where Church proudly led his daughter into his new home at 384 South Lauderdale Street. Mollie had known that her father was building a big house, but just how big she hadn't imagined. Three stories high, the house had fourteen rooms plus bathrooms, storerooms, a cellar, and a butler's pantry. Former slave Robert Church had grown so wealthy from his real estate holdings that he now owned a mansion, complete with stables for his horses.

Shortly after Mollie moved into her father's new home, he informed her of his plans. On January 1, 1885, he was going to marry Anna Wright. What did Mollie think?

Anna Wright was a family friend. A black school principal in Memphis, she was also a well-known pianist who had given Mollie music lessons years earlier. Mollie assured her father that she liked Anna and was happy for him. Robert Church then revealed his plans for Mollie. She needn't get a job, he told his daughter. She could live in his new house until she got married.

Mollie understood why her father didn't want her to work. At that time not many women had jobs, and very few wealthy women worked

Robert Church's home at 384 South Lauderdale Street in Memphis.

outside the home. Robert Church wanted everyone to see that his daughter could go to parties, travel, and do what she pleased—just like rich white ladies. Many people in Mollie's position would have considered this a golden opportunity, especially since it would give her a chance to write. But Mollie refused her father's offer. She was about to turn twenty-one, she was a college graduate, and she wanted to make her own way in the world. Robert Church was jolted. Used to giving orders, he felt wounded that his daughter wouldn't obey his wishes.

She didn't leave right away. Mollie stayed for her father's wedding, which took place as planned on New Year's Day of 1885. Mollie remained in the mansion with her father and his new bride until the middle of that year. By then her plans were formed. She would go to New York City and look for a teaching position, with the idea of writing in her free time. Until the moment of Mollie's departure her father hoped she would change her mind, but one summer day in 1885 she kissed him good-bye and boarded the train.

Mary Church was eager and a little scared as she set out to start a life of her own.

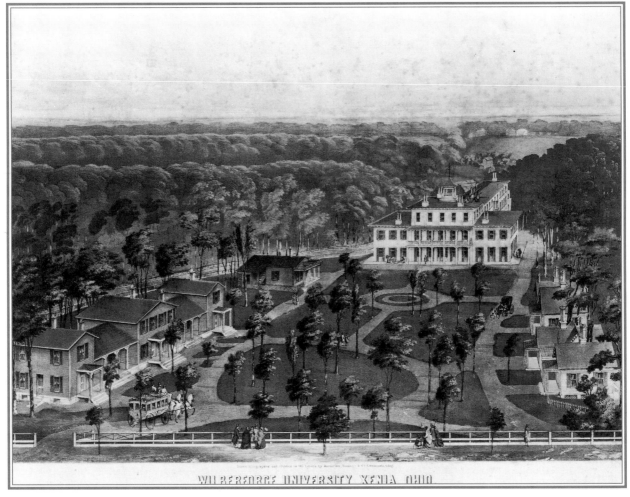

WILBERFORCE UNIVERSITY XENIA OHIO

Wilberforce University in the mid-1800s.

5

"The Welfare of My Race"

Mollie had done a great deal of soul-searching during the year she had spent in her father's house. She had decided to become a teacher because, as she explained, she wanted to do something to "promote the welfare of my race."

Soon after arriving at her mother's home in New York, Mollie applied to teach in several schools for black students. At least two offered her positions. She accepted an offer from Wilberforce University. That fall she traveled to Wilberforce, located near Dayton, in southwest Ohio. She was surprised to find that although the students were black, nearly all the teachers were white. She was astonished to learn all that was expected of her for forty dollars a month.

Mollie was to teach reading, writing, French, and geology. She was expected to serve as the faculty secretary. She also had to play the organ for church services Sunday mornings and evenings and help direct the choir one night a week. What made her job especially difficult was that, having just turned twenty-two, Miss Church was younger than many of her students. Moreover, she knew hardly anything about geology and had taken only one year of French at Oberlin. She had to stay up late each night just to remain a step ahead of her students.

Her father was so angry with Mollie that during her first year at Wilberforce he sent her just one letter—and that was to reprimand her

Louisa Ayers Church (on right) with her children, Mollie and Thomas.

for going off to teach. Never before had her father been this upset with her. Mollie felt bad, but as she wrote, "I knew I had done right to use my training in behalf of my race."

Following the 1885–1886 school year, Mollie spent the first half of summer vacation in New York with her mother, then headed to Memphis to make up with her father. Instead of asking her father if she could visit, she sent him a telegram from a stop along the way announcing that she would arrive at the Memphis station early the next morning. When she stepped off the train at five A.M., her father was waiting for her on the platform with open arms. She was as stubborn as he was, Robert Church told his daughter, and he promised not to discourage her from teaching anymore. He kept his word and, at the end of the summer, sent her back to Wilberforce with his best wishes.

Mollie had finished her second year at Wilberforce University when the Washington, D.C., Board of Education offered her a job teaching Latin at the M Street Colored High School. Wedged between the states of Maryland and Virginia, the nation's capital, like other Southern cities, had separate schools for black and white students. Mollie was excited at the prospect of teaching at what was considered the country's top high school for black students. By the late summer of 1887 she had accepted the offer and moved to Washington.

Washington, D.C., around the time Mollie Church moved there.

She had been in the city just a day or two when people began to tell her about the chairman of the M Street Colored High School's Latin department. Robert Heberton Terrell had been born a slave on a plantation in Orange, Virginia, in 1857. Besides laboring in the fields, Robert's father had made shoes for the plantation slaves. Working at night by candlelight, he needed a long time to complete a single pair of shoes. One of Robert Terrell's favorite stories was of how as a child he hopped around the plantation wearing one shoe while waiting for his father to finish the other.

Freed by the Union's victory in the Civil War, Robert's family moved to Washington, D.C., along with thousands of other former slaves seeking opportunities in the capital. It had been against the law to teach slaves to read or write, so it wasn't until the age of ten that Robert first learned the alphabet. He then attended Washington's public schools.

For many years schools in Washington, D.C., were segregated. This is a white school of the 1890s . . .

. . . and this is Dunbar High School, formerly the M Street Colored High School.

At sixteen Robert Terrell left home and moved to Boston, Massachusetts, to further his education. While attending schools to prepare for college, he supported himself by waiting tables, teaching ex-slaves to read and write, shoveling snow, and running errands. He entered Harvard University when he was twenty-three. Robert graduated in 1884, the same year Mollie received her diploma from Oberlin. He was the first African American to deliver the Harvard graduation speech.

Young Mr. Terrell was extremely ambitious. His goal was to become an attorney. In addition to heading the M Street Colored High School's Latin department, he attended night classes at Howard University's law school in Washington.

When she first arrived in the nation's capital, Mollie lived at the home of Dr. John Francis and his wife. Dr. Francis was a black member of the city's Board of Education. On her first Sunday afternoon in the city, Mollie was sitting on their doorstep when a tall, well-dressed young man approached the house. From what she had been told, Mollie knew he was the head of the Latin department. She jumped to her feet, ran upstairs, and shouted to Mrs. Francis, "Mr. Terrell has come!"

Mrs. Francis burst out laughing at Mollie's excitement. She was flustered because she had been sitting alone and there was no one to introduce her to Mr. Terrell, the young teacher explained. Mrs. Francis came downstairs and introduced the pair.

Soon the school year began and Robert Terrell assigned Mollie to teach first- and second-year Latin classes. She had received a strong background in Latin at Oberlin and was an outstanding teacher. From the start she was aware that her department chairman sought opportunities to speak to her. Occasionally, Mr. Terrell invited Mollie to take over his senior class. And whenever he came across a difficult Latin sentence, he would tell his students, "I'll ask Miss Church and see what she thinks about it."

He'd consult Miss Church after school. The next day he would tell his class her opinion. The students would exchange knowing glances, as if to say, "We all knew you would think your assistant was right."

Everyone knew that Mr. Terrell was sweet on Miss Church. She liked him, too, but wasn't sure what to do about it. Young men and women of that period courted by taking Sunday walks, attending concerts, or sitting and talking in the young woman's parlor. If they liked each other, they might marry after a brief courtship. In an era when the typical American woman was twenty-two and the typical man twenty-six at the time of a first marriage, Mollie was twenty-four and Robert was thirty. They were certainly at the "marrying age."

But there was a problem. School systems in the 1800s had very strict rules for female teachers. Often, married women were not allowed to teach—partly because schools were afraid they would become pregnant and leave in the middle of the year. Moreover, if a teacher showed what was considered a little too much of her legs or was seen entering a man's house alone, she risked losing her job for "immoral behavior." Many teachers were fired simply because of gossip that they were romantically involved with a colleague. Mollie didn't want to be the subject of rumors, and she wasn't ready for marriage, so she had little to do with Robert Heberton Terrell outside of school.

Robert Heberton Terrell.

Before the school year ended, Mollie's father made her an offer. He would pay for her to take an extensive European tour and would accompany her part of the way. She could even remain in Europe for a year to study if she wanted. Mollie saw this as a chance to see the world, broaden her education, be with her father, and take a breather from Robert Terrell. She obtained a leave of absence from the high school and accepted her father's proposal.

In the summer of 1888, Mollie and her father met in New York and sailed for Europe on the *City of Berlin*. The passengers included a sister of Harriet Beecher Stowe, author of the famous anti-slavery novel *Uncle Tom's Cabin*. Isabella Beecher Hooker was impressed by Mollie, and she wrote letters of introduction for her to prominent people in Europe.

Mollie and her father traveled through England and France for several weeks. Robert Church then had to return home to business and his new family. He and Anna now had two children of their own: Robert Jr., who was three, and Annette, who was just a year old. Although Robert Church had told Mollie that she could remain in Europe, his eyes filled with tears as he stood with her on the platform in Paris, waiting for the train that would start him homeward. He begged his daughter to change her mind and return to the States with him, but she was determined to stay. Her father kissed her good-bye and boarded the train.

Mollie recovered from her father's departure within minutes. Alone in Paris without a care in the world, she was "bubbling over with enthusiasm and youth," she recalled in her autobiography.

Mary Church spent two years in Europe, studying literature and languages while traveling through France, Switzerland, Germany, and Italy. Ever since learning a little German from her childhood playmates, Mollie had shown a gift for languages. In Europe she became almost as fluent in French and German as she was in English, and she also learned to speak Italian. Her mother and brother, Thomas, joined her for a few weeks on her travels. Ordinarily, Louisa couldn't have afforded such a costly trip, but she had won fifteen thousand dollars—about $300,000 in today's money—in a lottery and had decided to spend some of that money touring Europe with her daughter and son.

Mary Church went to Europe in 1888.

The three of them visited the Paris Exposition of 1889, for which the Eiffel Tower had been built. At this world's fair Mollie was introduced to an African prince who had been educated in Paris. Thanks to Mrs. Hooker's letters of introduction, Mollie met many other people during her two years abroad. Two European men proposed marriage to her.

The first was a penniless pianist from Austria who admitted that he wanted to marry her for her money. Mollie turned him down, saying that marrying without love was a sin. The second was a wealthy German baron who, without discussing it with Mollie, wrote to her father asking for her hand in marriage. Robert Church answered that he wouldn't consent to his daughter marrying a foreigner and living in Europe. Of course Mollie would have married the baron had she loved him, but she didn't, so she rejected his proposal, too. Four thousand miles from home, Mollie found her thoughts drifting back to a certain high school Latin teacher.

One day while walking through Berlin, Germany, Mollie felt another tug on her heart that surprised her. She was passing the American consulate when she saw a U.S. flag waving in the wind. Her eyes moistened and a lump formed in her throat as she stared at the Stars and Stripes. Half a century later, she recalled her thoughts at that moment:

> *It's my country. I have a perfect right to love it and I will. My African ancestors helped to build and enrich it for nearly three hundred years, while they were shackled body and soul in the most cruel bondage the world has ever seen. My African ancestors suffered and died for it as slaves and they have fought, bled, and died for it as soldiers in every war which it has waged. It has been cruel to us in the past and it is often unjust to us now, but it is my country after all, and with all its faults I love it still.*

In the spring of 1890—a few weeks before Idaho and Wyoming achieved statehood—Mollie boarded a steamship in England and sailed for home. After landing in New York, she accompanied her mother to Marietta, Ohio, to attend Thomas's graduation from Marietta College on July 2. From there Mollie went to Memphis to visit her father. Somewhere along the line a letter from Robert Terrell caught up with her. Mollie's two-year leave of absence had expired. If she wanted to return to the M Street Colored High School, she had better tell the superintendent of colored schools her intentions.

Mollie notified her superintendent that she would like to return to the high school. She was reappointed to her teaching position. By the late summer of 1890 she was back in Washington, preparing for the coming school year.

Blacks weren't allowed in Memphis's public parks, so around 1900 Robert Church built Church's Park and Auditorium for African Americans; many concerts were held there.

Mr. Terrell "Goes to Church"

Mollie was assigned to teach Latin and German. Having let her slip away once, Robert Terrell was not about to let it happen again. His feelings for her—and hers for him—were now so obvious that the whole school knew there was a budding romance between them. Upon entering her classroom, Mollie would sometimes find that a student had written on her blackboard:

MR. TERRELL IS CERTAINLY GETTING GOOD. HE USED TO GO TO DANCES, BUT NOW HE GOES TO CHURCH.

Robert Terrell had been busy in Mollie's absence. In 1889 he had graduated at the top of his class from Howard University's law school. Despite his love for teaching, sometime before January 1891 Robert took a higher-paying job in the U.S. Treasury Department. By then he had asked Mollie to marry him and she had said yes. Like the German baron, Robert Terrell wrote to Mollie's father, only he did so *after* she had accepted his proposal:

> *Washington, D.C*
> *Jan. 6, 1891*

My Dear Sir:
>   *The privilege I take in sending you this letter is warranted by such a sacred relationship between your daughter and myself*

that I do not feel that it is necessary for me to apologize for it. With Miss Mollie's free consent and approval I write to ask of you her hand in marriage. On our part this is no hasty step. We feel that we know each other thoroughly [but Mollie wants] your approving word. Begging a reply at your earliest convenience,

I am, yours sincerely,
Robt. H. Terrell

Robert Church gave his blessing, and invitations for the upcoming wedding went out to friends and relatives:

Mr. Robert R. Church
requests your presence
at the marriage of his daughter
Mary Eliza
to
Mr. Robert Heberton Terrell.
Wednesday evening, October twenty eighth,
at six o'clock
Lauderdale Street
Memphis, Tenn.

The wedding was held as scheduled at Mollie's father's house on the evening of October 28, 1891. A large number of guests enjoyed the feast that Robert Church put on, then danced to what the *Memphis Commercial Appeal* called the "sensuous strains of Joe Hall's orchestra, which, hidden in an alcove, made the air sweet with its beautiful music."

Mollie had just one disappointment. Feeling that her presence at her former husband's home would be awkward, Louisa Ayers Church didn't attend her daughter's wedding. While honeymooning in New York, the couple visited Louisa, who said that on the evening of the wedding she had dressed exactly as she would have had she been there, and that at the exact time of the marriage vows she had pretended she was listening to the actual ceremony.

The newlyweds rented a two-room apartment in Washington. Mollie was forced to resign from teaching because she was married. Robert missed teaching so much that he quit his job with the Treasury Department and returned to the M Street Colored High School, where he became the principal.

Mollie and Robert were deeply in love, but their first years of marriage were filled with sorrow. Over five years they had three babies, each of whom died shortly after birth. Besides mourning their loss, they felt bitter knowing that the infants might have lived had they not been born in inferior Jim Crow medical facilities. For example, their third baby had been placed in a makeshift incubator and had died two days after birth. Mollie was tormented by the thought that her baby might have survived in a regular incubator, like those available to white people.

To make things worse, in the spring of 1892 Mollie received distressing news from Memphis about Thomas Moss, a friend from her childhood. Moss and two other black men had opened a grocery store. Jealous of their success, a white grocer organized a mob that stormed the rival store, attacked Moss and his partners, and then shot them dead. This brutal triple slaying inspired another friend of Mollie's, Ida B. Wells, to begin a lifelong crusade to end lynching—the murder of people by mobs, often for racial reasons.

Her babies' deaths and the murder of her childhood friend combined to crush Mollie's spirits. She sank into deep depressions on and off during the 1890s. Her physical health also broke down to the point that her family feared for her life. In the summer of 1892 Mollie's father sent Robert Terrell a letter rejoicing over Mollie's recovery from a serious health crisis.

New interests helped lift her spirits. Now that she could no longer teach in the public schools, she had no way to promote the welfare of her race. Mary Church Terrell, which was how she was becoming known, renewed her commitment to her people as her health improved. In June of 1892 she and a few other women organized the Colored Woman's League of

Ida B. Wells waged a lifelong crusade against lynching.

Washington, which declared that its purpose was "to promote the best interests of the colored people in any direction that suggests itself."

The Colored Woman's League of Washington worked on many fronts. It offered night school classes for adults, with Mollie herself teaching English literature and German. The league opened two kindergarten classes for the city's black children and created a day nursery to provide working mothers with a safe place to leave their children. The league also began a sewing class and a kitchen gardening course for young women. Mary Church Terrell's work with the Colored Woman's League of Washington launched her on a career with black women's organizations that was to span sixty years.

Many other black women's groups were being founded across the country. Chicago's first civic club for black women was created in 1893 and named the Ida B. Wells Club for its founder. Between 1892 and 1896 similar clubs were begun in Boston, Massachusetts; New Orleans, Louisiana; Providence, Rhode Island; Knoxville, Tennessee; Pittsburgh, Pennsylvania; New York City; Omaha, Nebraska; and Jefferson City, Missouri. Largely forgotten today, these organizations were not only the country's first civic clubs for black women, they paved the way for the modern civil rights movement.

Their members fought lynching and Jim Crow, and worked to improve educational and job opportunities for African Americans.

Her prominence in the Colored Woman's League of Washington opened doors for Mary Church Terrell. One of the deadliest years for lynchings in U.S. history was 1892, the year Thomas Moss was murdered. At least 230 Americans, more than 160 of them black, were killed by mobs that year. In 1892 or early 1893 Mollie and fellow Washingtonian Frederick Douglass requested a meeting with President Benjamin Harrison to discuss lynching. Had she acted as an individual, she might have been ignored, but as a leader of the Colored Woman's League of Washington, twenty-nine-year-old Mary Church Terrell was invited to accompany seventy-five-year-old Frederick Douglass to the White House.

According to an *Ebony* magazine article Mary Church Terrell wrote sixty years later, Douglass "implored" President Harrison to use his power to end lynching. Then Mrs. Terrell said, "Please, Mr. President, do something at once to stop the lynching of Negroes in the South!" But Harrison did little to

President Benjamin Harrison.

Mary Church Terrell, within a few years of her marriage.

combat lynching, which finally died out in the 1930s, in large because of the efforts of Ida B. Wells. By visiting the president, however, Terrell and Douglass helped attract national attention to the problem.

Her role in the Colored Woman's League of Washington also helped Mary Church Terrell achieve a historic first. In 1895 she became the first black woman appointed to the Washington, D.C., Board of Education. During her eleven years (1895–1901 and 1906–1911) on the board, Mrs. Terrell attended meetings, visited schools, went to Congress to request funds for salaries and building repairs, and helped hire teachers for the black schools. She was barraged by people seeking teaching jobs. For example, Charles W. Chesnutt, author of *The Conjure Woman* and renowned as the first major African American fiction writer, sent a letter to Mrs. Terrell asking that his son-in-law be appointed as a high school teacher.

One of her greatest achievements as a Board of Education member came in 1897. Frederick Douglass had died two years earlier at the age of seventy-eight. Washington's black schools should set aside a day to honor Douglass, Mary Church Terrell suggested. The capital's black schools began celebrating Douglass Day in 1897. Held on or around February 14—his birthday—the day featured songs, speeches, and essays about the great leader. Douglass Day may have inspired Mary Church Terrell's friend Carter G. Woodson to establish Negro History Week in 1926. This in turn grew into Black History Month, now celebrated each February.

Mary Church Terrell also wanted to establish another special "day." She and her husband loved animals and had a dog named Nogi. Mrs. Terrell proposed that Washington schools—black and white—set aside a day when students would be reminded to be kind to animals. For years she lobbied for Animal Day, but the Board of Education never approved this idea.

Meanwhile, the achievements of black women's organizations that had sprung up around the country showed that there was strength in numbers. Mary Church Terrell, Josephine St. Pierre Ruffin of Boston, and other black women decided to unite the local clubs into a single powerful national organization. In July of 1896 black women representing civic clubs from across the United States met in Washington, D.C. At this gathering more than one hundred black women's clubs, including the Colored Woman's League of Washington, joined together to form a new, giant federation, the National Association of Colored Women (NACW).

Who would be its first president? Mary Church Terrell, widely considered to be the country's best-educated black woman, was a leading candidate. But again and again the vote of the fourteen-person committee assigned to elect a president resulted in a 7–7 tie. Finally, on the evening of July 21, 1896, the deadlock was broken and Mrs. Terrell was elected.

In addition to her Board of Education responsibilities, Mary Church Terrell was now the first president of the leading organization for black women in the nation.

Booker T. Washington.

"Lifting As We Climb"

After Frederick Douglass died in 1895, African Americans divided into two camps over racial matters. Booker T. Washington, a former slave who had founded a black training school called Tuskegee Institute in Alabama, led the group that spoke of "uplifting the race." Washington and his followers believed that blacks should learn a trade and work at self-improvement, rather than complain a lot about segregation and other injustices. Admirers of Washington were called "Bookerites" for their leader, or "conservatives" for their slow and cautious approach on racial issues. They were also called "gradualists," because they hoped that as blacks proved their worth, whites would gradually accept them.

The other group didn't want to wait for justice and equality. They felt that African Americans had a right to fair play and should demand it. Called "militants" or "anti-Bookerites," this group included history professor W. E. B. Du Bois, who criticized Washington for accepting second-class citizenship, as well as Ida B. Wells, who vehemently fought lynching. The Black Power movement of more recent times evolved from this militant way of thinking.

The National Association of Colored Women adhered to Booker T. Washington's ideas of gradually "uplifting the race." The motto Mary Church Terrell coined for the organization—"Lifting as we climb"—reflected this. In "The Duty of the NACW to the Race," an article published in 1900,

W. E. B. Du Bois, a leading critic of Booker T. Washington's "gradualist" theory.

Mrs. Terrell wrote that the organization's goal was "to come into closer touch with the masses of our women," "to uplift and reclaim them," and "to elevate the race." Booker T. Washington had a direct connection with the NACW. His wife, Margaret Murray Washington, was an NACW officer under Mrs. Terrell and later became the organization's president.

At the NACW's first convention, held in Nashville, Tennessee, in September of 1897, President Terrell said that above all she wanted the NACW to help black children. "Surely nothing can be nearer our hearts than the children, many of whose sad and dark lives we might brighten and bless," she told the delegates sent from around the country by black women's clubs. "It is kindergartens we need, free kindergartens in every city and hamlet of this broad land, if the children are to receive from us what it is our duty to give. . . . More than any other race in this country, we should implant feelings of self-respect and pride in our children, whose spirits are crushed and hearts saddened by cruel prejudice."

Much of what Mrs. Terrell achieved as president of the NACW from 1896 to 1901 was for the sake of children. Under her leadership, the NACW opened kindergartens and day nurseries. It created mothers' clubs to teach parenting skills and children's clubs to provide activities for young people. Mrs. Terrell began *National Notes*, a monthly newsletter that kept members in touch, and she wrote newspaper and magazine articles about NACW projects across the country. She was also a great fundraiser, as this letter asking wealthy white people to help establish kindergartens shows:

Newspaper sketch of Mary Church Terrell at the time she was president of the NACW.

NATIONAL ASSOCIATION OF COLORED WOMEN
MARY CHURCH TERRELL, PRES., WASHINGTON, D.C.
MRS. BOOKER T. WASHINGTON, CHAIRMAN
EXECUTIVE COMMITTEE, TUSKEGEE, ALA.

Feb. 17, 1900

The colored women of the country are trying to improve the condition of our people. We believe that by reaching our children we shall do the most good. We are trying to establish kindergartens especially for the little waifs of the South. We have founded several such institutions from which encouraging reports have come. We are greatly in need of means now with which to continue our work. May I not ask you to assist us? If you will establish a kindergarten for colored children in the South, we shall name it [for you]. The cost will not be great, and it will do untold good to the poor little unfortunates who need it most.

I am very truly yours,
Mary Church Terrell

The NACW's first president took great pleasure in her work. Helping her people, especially the children, made her happy. She also looked forward to the national conventions, which were held in Nashville in 1897, Chicago in 1899, and Buffalo, New York, in 1901. For weeks before a convention, she worked on her speech and planned a schedule that would allow delegates from across the country to tell what their local clubs were doing.

Her NACW activities helped take her mind off the loss of her three babies. She even began to think of the organization as her child. In her article "The Duty of the NACW to the Race," Mrs. Terrell wrote:

An infant of but three years is this organization, over which I have had the honor to preside. . . . So tenderly has this child of the organized womanhood of the race been nurtured. . . . that it comes before you today a child hale, hearty, and strong, of which its fond mothers have every reason to be proud.

Meanwhile, Mollie's family life had begun to change. In 1893 her husband passed the bar exam. Robert Terrell resigned as a high school principal and entered law practice. A few years later—thanks partly to his wife's connections—he received a major appointment as a judge.

Theodore Roosevelt, the nation's president from 1901 to 1909, consulted Booker T. Washington on matters relating to African Americans. The president also sought his recommendations when appointing black people to federal posts. In 1902, at Washington's urging, President Roosevelt appointed Robert Terrell to be the first African American judge of the Municipal Court of the District of Columbia. Although Robert Terrell had outstanding credentials—he was a graduate of

This cartoon ridiculed Judge Robert Terrell simply because he was black; it was created by and for white bigots opposed to blacks holding any position of importance.

Harvard and of the Howard University law school—undoubtedly Mary's friendship with Booker T. Washington and his wife helped Judge Terrell obtain his appointment.

Robert Terrell earned a reputation as an outstanding judge. James C. McReynolds, the nation's attorney general under President Woodrow Wilson, called him "undoubtedly the best municipal judge that Washington has ever had." Every four years Judge Terrell had to be renominated by the president and approved by the U.S. Senate. Although his presidential nominations came without fail, Judge Terrell was confirmed by the Senate only with great difficulty.

Some senators, particularly those from the South, would have voted against a black man being named dogcatcher, let alone a municipal judge of the nation's capital. Had Mary Church Terrell spoken out strongly against segregation or done anything to antagonize whites, her husband might

Robert and Mary Church Terrell once lived in this house (half of which has been demolished) at 326 T Street N.W. in Washington, D.C.

Robert and Mary Church Terrell's daughters, Mary (on left) and Phyllis.

have lost enough votes in the Senate to have his confirmation defeated. So it may have been for the sake of Robert's career that she seemed to favor Booker T. Washington's approach for many years. Although she became a little more outspoken in the early 1900s, Mollie avoided major controversies as long as her husband was alive.

In 1898 Mary and Robert Terrell finally began the family they had long wanted. On April 2, at the age of thirty-four, Mary had her fourth baby. Unlike the first three, this child survived. The couple named her Phyllis, for Phillis Wheatley, a Boston slave who had become the first major African American poet. Phyllis was an only child for two years; then suddenly she had a sister four years older than she. Around 1894 Mary Church Terrell's brother, Thomas, had become the father of a little girl named Mary Louise.

The identity of Mary Louise's mother is unknown. For reasons that Mary Church Terrell never explained, she and Robert adopted Thomas's daughter sometime around 1900, when the girl was about six years old.

Mary Church Terrell's term as NACW president expired in 1901. In recognition of all she had done for the organization, Mrs. Terrell was voted "honorary president for life." She remained active in the NACW for the next half century, but never as intensely as during her five-year presidency.

After renting a small apartment at the start of their marriage, the Terrells bought a small house near Howard University. From there they moved into a larger house in the same neighborhood, a gift to them from Mary's father. Around the time of Phyllis's birth, Mary's mother, Louisa, moved from New York City into this house. Louisa would live with her daughter and her family for about the last fifteen years of her life. During these later years Louisa took up painting, with a special interest in such subjects as birds, butterflies, and flowers. She painted on a variety of surfaces besides canvas, including food trays and screens used as room dividers.

At the beginning of the twentieth century, radio and movies were just being invented. Television didn't yet exist. Plays and concerts were popular kinds of entertainment. Audiences also attended lectures on subjects ranging from the latest books to the possibility of life on Mars. As NACW president, Mary Church Terrell had occasionally presented lectures. Then, in about 1903, a lecture bureau asked her to travel through the country speaking about racial issues for fifteen dollars a talk.

Mary saw this as another opportunity to help her people. It was also a chance to earn some money, for she had served as a Board of Education member and as NACW president without pay. In today's money, fifteen dollars a lecture was worth about three hundred dollars—a rather tempting offer. Besides, for five years starting in 1901 she was no longer on the Board of Education and had become a full-time wife and mother. She was dying to get out of the house! Her mother agreed to care for the girls. Insisting only that her tours be limited to three weeks at a time, Mary Church Terrell signed a contract, beginning what would become a thirty-year career as a lecturer.

Mrs. Terrell traveled by train from town to town. In the South she had to

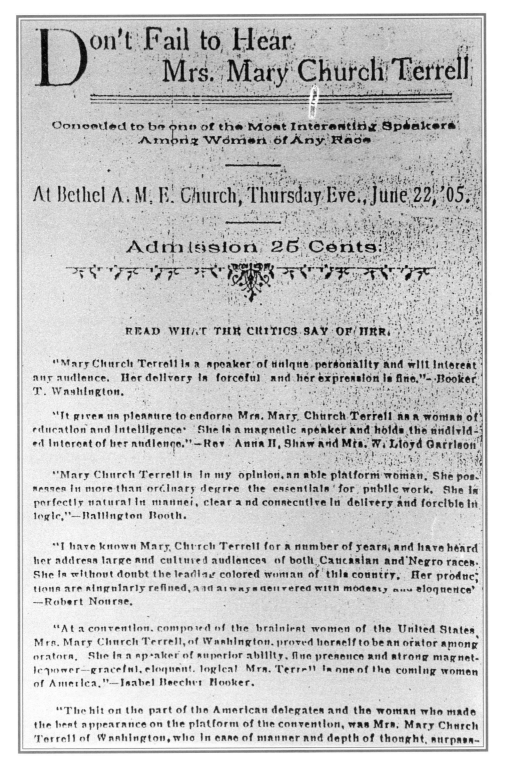

Don't Fail to Hear
Mrs. Mary Church Terrell

Conceded to be one of the Most Interesting Speakers
Among Women of Any Race

At Bethel A. M. E. Church, Thursday Eve., June 22, '05.

Admission 25 Cents.

READ WHAT THE CRITICS SAY OF HER.

"Mary Church Terrell is a speaker of unique personality and will interest any audience. Her delivery is forceful and her expression is fine."— Booker T. Washington.

"It gives us pleasure to endorse Mrs. Mary Church Terrell as a woman of education and intelligence. She is a magnetic speaker and holds the undivided interest of her audience."—Rev. Anna H. Shaw and Mrs. W. Lloyd Garrison.

"Mary Church Terrell is in my opinion an able platform woman. She possesses in more than ordinary degree the essentials for public work. She is perfectly natural in manner, clear and consecutive in delivery and forcible in logic."—Ballington Booth.

"I have known Mary Church Terrell for a number of years, and have heard her address large and cultured audiences of both Caucasian and Negro races. She is without doubt the leading colored woman of this country. Her productions are singularly refined, and always delivered with modesty and eloquence."—Robert Nourse.

"At a convention, composed of the brainiest women of the United States, Mrs. Mary Church Terrell, of Washington, proved herself to be an orator among orators. She is a speaker of superior ability, fine presence and strong magnetic power—graceful, eloquent, logical. Mrs. Terrell is one of the coming women of America."—Isabel Beecher Hooker.

"The hit on the part of the American delegates and the woman who made the best appearance on the platform of the convention, was Mrs. Mary Church Terrell of Washington, who in ease of manner and depth of thought, surpass-

Advertisement for a Mary Church Terrell lecture.

ride in the Jim Crow "colored car," stay at Jim Crow hotels, and eat at Jim Crow restaurants. Some days she went twenty-four hours without eating, because no restaurant in a town would serve a black person. Prior to her arrival in a town, leaflets, such as the following, would be passed out:

GREAT LECTURER!
MRS. MARY CHURCH-TERRELL

One of the world's Greatest Negro Women

You cannot afford to miss this rare treat.
This lecture is given under the auspices of the
Oklahoma City Federation of Negro Women's Clubs.

Avery A.M.E. Church Friday Night, May 3rd, 1912

ADMISSION: ADULTS 25 CENTS CHILDREN 10 CENTS

She spoke in churches, auditoriums, city halls, tents, schools, and club headquarters—to audiences as large as four thousand people. Her talks were upbeat. One of her most popular lectures, "A Bright Side of a Dark Subject," chronicled black people's achievements. Another, "The Progress of Colored Women," reviewed the success of black women as teachers, club leaders, and founders of orphanages and homes for the elderly.

Mrs. Terrell attracted both white and black audiences—although rarely at the same event. White people who had never met any African Americans except perhaps cooks or gardeners came away from her talks amazed at what they had learned about black history. Often the same people who wouldn't let her into their hotels or restaurants had some of their prejudice peeled away by the eloquent lecturer from the nation's capital.

Black listeners were filled with pride as they heard her speak. Many of them hadn't known that their people had produced Crispus Attucks, one of the first Americans to die in the Revolutionary era; Benjamin Banneker, the astronomer and surveyor who had helped lay out Washington, D.C.; or the poets Phillis Wheatley and Paul Laurence Dunbar. For ten cents, thousands of children received a lesson in black history from Mrs. Terrell that they never forgot. What were the chances that they would ever again meet a black woman who spoke to presidents and had actually known Frederick Douglass?

Thanks to a daily diary that she was keeping by 1905, we know about her grueling lecture schedule. She was so popular that her fee soon rose to twenty-five dollars per speech. With dozens of groups clamoring for her, she abandoned her three-weeks-at-a-time rule. In the spring of 1908 forty-four-year-old Mary Church Terrell made a seven-week trip. Leaving home on March 26, she began with a visit to her father in Memphis on March 28 and then continued with a speaking tour to some twenty-five cities and towns in the South and Southwest. She spoke on April 2 in Little Rock and on April 3 in Hot Springs, Arkansas, but then had a rough experience on April 5 in Fort Smith. Her diary entry for that day reads:

> *Left for Ft. Smith, Ark. Started on the Jim Crow car and had to go the entire day without food—was deathly sick when I reached Ft. Smith about seven having had nothing to eat since five o'clock in the morning—I fell into the bed after sipping a cup of tea thoroughly discouraged after learning that the engagement had been called off.*

She then spoke in the following places:

April 7: Pine Bluff, Arkansas
April 10: Meridian, Mississippi
April 11: Jackson, Mississippi
April 14: Shreveport, Louisiana
April 15: Marshall, Texas
April 16: Dallas, Texas
April 19: Fort Worth, Texas
April 20: Austin, Texas
April 21: Waco, Texas
April 22: Houston, Texas
April 23: Galveston, Texas
April 24: New Orleans, Louisiana

April 27: Mobile, Alabama
April 28: Baton Rouge, Louisiana
April 30: Natchez, Mississippi
  May 1: Vicksburg, Mississippi
  May 4: Paris, Texas
  May 5: Gainesville, Texas
  May 6: Ardmore, Oklahoma
  May 7: Oklahoma City, Oklahoma
  May 8: Guthrie, Oklahoma

Although more pronounced in the South, segregation was practiced in many places in the North, too; this sign was on a whites-only restaurant in Lancaster, Ohio, during the 1930s.

She headed for home on May 9. By May 10 she was in Kansas City, Missouri, for breakfast and in Chicago for dinner. Mrs. Terrell left Chicago on May 11. The next day she arrived in Washington after forty-seven days on the road.

Jim Crow laws were spreading like a cancer throughout the South at the time Mrs. Terrell set out to lecture. By 1902 blacks had been deprived of the vote so extensively that no African American sat in either the U.S. Congress or any state legislature, North or South. States and cities passed Jim Crow laws for every aspect of life. Between the late 1800s and 1907 Georgia, North Carolina, Virginia, Louisiana, Arkansas, South Carolina, Tennessee, Mississippi, Maryland, Florida, and Oklahoma passed laws requiring blacks to sit in Jim Crow sections of streetcars. Georgia adopted a Separate Park Law in 1905. In 1909, the year after Mary Church Terrell lectured there, Mobile, Alabama, passed a law requiring black residents to be off the streets by ten P.M. By 1914 six towns in Texas, five in Oklahoma, and two in Alabama had laws forbidding blacks to live within their borders. The Oklahoma legislature decided in 1915 that telephone companies must provide "separate booths for white and colored patrons." North Carolina and Florida had laws requiring that textbooks used by white and black schoolchildren be kept separate. Sixteen states had laws forbidding blacks to marry whites, some as late as 1967.

Generally, a person was considered African American if he or she had *any* black ancestors. Mrs. Terrell was relatively light-skinned, but she didn't want to try to "pass for white" for two reasons. She was proud of her African heritage. Also, if caught trying to "pass" in the South, she might have been sent to jail. Still, now and then she was mistaken for white anyway.

On one occasion, while she was headed to speak in Paris, Texas, her train stopped unexpectedly for the night in Texarkana, Arkansas. "What shall I do?" she asked the conductor. "I am acquainted with no one here. Where can I stop tonight? I can't stop at a hotel in Texarkana." Like many other southern towns, Texarkana had been the scene of several brutal lynchings. At least four black people were lynched there between 1889 and 1906.

She was so smudged with smoke and dust from her day of travel that the conductor thought she was white. "Certainly you can," he said. "There's a fine hotel just across from the station."

Burdened with a heavy suitcase, not knowing where else to go, she entered the whites-only hotel. The desk clerk didn't question her race, so she registered under her own name and ate a quick dinner in the dining room before heading to her room. Once in bed, she began to worry. She had been speaking in the South for a few weeks. What if the desk clerk had seen her name in the newspaper and figured out who she was? What if another hotel guest had recognized her? She finally fell asleep, but in the middle of the night she was awakened by a knock at her door.

She began trembling, certain that the police had come to throw her in jail or that a mob intended to beat her up or lynch her. She decided that if a mob burst in on her, she would run to the balcony and jump to the ground.

There was a second knock, and then a third. Finally, she called out, "Who is it? What do you want?"

"Lady," a voice asked, "did you ring for a pitcher of water?"

"No, I did not!" she answered, relieved that it was just a bellboy who had come to the wrong room.

If anybody at the hotel suspected that she was black, they made no issue

Lynchings often attracted huge mobs; this photograph shows a crowd gathered for a lynching in a town in Texas.

of it, for the next day she checked out with no problem and continued on to her speaking engagement.

However, an incident in Dover, Delaware, showed just how quickly trouble could develop for a black traveler. The man who was supposed to meet her at the train station had not arrived, so Mrs. Terrell went to a telephone booth to call him. By mistake she looked in the section of the phone book for Wilmington, Delaware, rather than Dover, and could not find the number she wanted.

Approaching the ticket window, she said, "I am a stranger here, and I am trying to reach Mr. Ross, whom I expected to meet me. I cannot find his name in the telephone directory. Have you any idea how I could reach him?"

The ticket agent scowled and said, "Go look in the telephone directory."

"I have already looked there before I came to you, and I cannot find his name," she answered.

The ticket agent refused to help her. "Get away from this window," he ordered, "and don't bother me anymore!"

Mrs. Terrell began to explain again that she couldn't find the name she needed, but the man roared, "Get away or I'll have you arrested!"

"For what?" she asked, shocked by the threat.

In a rage the ticket agent called the police and asked them to arrest a black woman in the station who was being disorderly. Mrs. Terrell didn't wait for the police to arrive. She stepped into a cab and asked the driver whether he knew where a black paperhanger named Ross lived. The driver took her to Mr. Ross's home; however, Mr. Ross had already left to pick her up at the station. She had to wait on his porch for an hour before he came home.

He had heard about the incident at the station, Mr. Ross told Mrs. Terrell, warning her that there might be more trouble. That night two railroad detectives came to the theater where Mrs. Terrell was speaking to arrest her, but changed their minds once they realized she was famous. Nevertheless, the ticket agent persisted. Mrs. Terrell was forced to hire a lawyer, turn herself in for arrest, post bail, and appear in court. Only after several months of wrangling was the disorderly-conduct charge dropped.

"This experience was very valuable to me," Mary Church Terrell wrote in her autobiography. "It proved to me how easily a serious charge based upon a trivial incident may be trumped up against a colored woman or man."

She knew that, were she a few shades darker, her experience at the Texarkana hotel might not have ended so well; were she not a well-known person who could hire a lawyer, she might have been locked in the Dover jail merely for asking a ticket agent for help.

Mary Church Terrell.

"I Have Done So Little"

Mary Church Terrell felt that as one of America's most famous black women, she represented her entire race. Whites who knew no other black people might base their opinions of African Americans on their impressions of her. So when out in public, she dressed like a fashion model, spoke like an English teacher, and carried herself with the bearing of a queen. Mrs. Terrell was so proper that people who didn't know her sometimes found her old-fashioned, or even cool and aloof. Fortunately, we have her diaries and letters, which reveal a very different woman.

She was extremely affectionate toward close friends and family. Throughout their married life, Mary and her husband remained very devoted to one another. When she was traveling, one of the first things she did was write a letter to Robert. She addressed these letters to "My darling Husband" or to "My darling Hubbykin," and sometimes signed them "Your affectionate Wifie." A letter she wrote in late November 1900 reveals her feelings toward Robert after nine years of marriage:

St. Louis, Mo.
Nov. 1900

My own Darling:
    This is Thanksgiving Day and while I am very, very happy here I should be so much happier at home with my own family.

I shall leave here tomorrow Friday morning at 8:30 and reach Washington at two in the afternoon [a few days later]. Just telephone and see whether the train is on time before you come down to the depot. I want you to be sure to be there. I want to see you so badly, my darling. It seems an age since I have been in your dear arms. I am getting more and more dependent upon you as I grow older. The room is full of company waiting for me downstairs, but I have run away for a minute to write this letter to you

She must have been suddenly called downstairs, because she didn't place the final period on her last sentence or close with her usual words of love.

She also found it consoling to tell her husband her problems, as in this letter from early 1905:

WHITE'S HOTEL
MASSENA, N.Y.

My darling Husband:

I have run against a terrible snag and as usual I am pouring out my woes to you. This is a strenuous life I'm leading, I tell you. It is anything but a snap, this lecture business. As a usual thing I have to get up and take five or six o'clock trains in the morning, when I've reached the place at which I have passed the night about 11 or 12. It is very wearing on the nerves indeed.

After discussing many things in this six-page letter, she closed by saying:

Kiss Phyllis thousands of times for me. Take lots of kisses for yourself.

> *Your affectionate Wife,*
> *Mollie*

Judge Robert Terrell, whom his wife affectionately referred to as "Hubbykin."

Perhaps because she had lost three babies, Mrs. Terrell was a very protective mother—what we might call a "worrywart." Phyllis and Mary couldn't take a breath without their mother worrying about them. When they were ill, she couldn't bear it. On New Year's Day of 1908 young Mary had her tonsils and adenoids removed. Although asked to leave the operating room, Mrs. Terrell insisted on staying with her daughter through the surgery. "The doctor wanted me to go out of the room," she wrote in her diary, "but I refused to do it and Mary urged me to remain. I had no intention of leaving." The next year, on September 5, Mrs. Terrell reported that Phippie, as she called Phyllis, had a high fever. "It worries me dreadfully when she is ill," she confessed.

She supervised her daughters' schoolwork and wanted them to get A's so badly that she helped them do their homework. "Have been helping Mary with her Latin which she hasn't studied at all," Mrs. Terrell wrote in her diary on November 23, 1909. "I am greatly disappointed to think she has no more pride." She sat in on their music lessons, too. At her eighth-grade graduation ceremony, thirteen-year-old Phippie played a piece on the violin. Not content to listen from the audience or let a fellow student accompany Phippie, Mrs. Terrell insisted on playing the piano accompaniment herself.

Mary Church Terrell had discovered a way to make sure that her daughters kept good company. She was one of their main playmates! Her December 27, 1909, diary entry describes an outing in which she pulled her daughters downtown on a sled:

> *In the afternoon the children and I took the sled downtown. Mary and I pulled P quite a distance, then P and I pulled Mary. For several blocks I held on to an ash wagon and pulled the sled.*

There is nothing unusual about a mother pulling her children on a sled, except that Mary Church Terrell was forty-six years old and Mary and Phyllis were fifteen and eleven at the time. But the most extreme example of Mrs. Terrell babying her daughters occurred in 1913, when the girls went to Oberlin, Ohio. There Phyllis enrolled in high school and Mary entered Oberlin College.

This was a rough time for Mrs. Terrell, whose mother had died not long before in their home in Washington. She accompanied her daughters to help them settle in Oberlin, but she was so reluctant to leave them that instead of staying a few days, she remained for several months. Young Mary was in the unusual situation of having her mother with her at college. Mrs. Terrell finally returned home after her daughters promised to write to her regularly. Among the many letters they sent her were these two:

136 W. College St.
Oberlin, Ohio
Nov. 26, 1913

Dear Mother,

Tomorrow night the faculty gives a party for its students. I am going and will wear my blue silk dress. My watch ran a half hour fast and I took it back to be refixed. We have met two lovely colored girls from Chicago. They seem just as sweet as can be. I think the girls and boys over to our boarding house are going on a [hike] tomorrow morning—Thanksgiven. Everything is going O.K. and I am practicing [music] well. Much love and many kisses. I am as ever your little daughter

Phyllis

P.S. Mary sends love also.

136 W. College St.
Oberlin, Ohio
April 2, 1914

Hello there, Mother dear:

Have just come home from English and have no other lessons to-day until four o'clock and that's basket-ball practice. It is now 9:30. The day is gray but I don't think it is going to rain. Tomorrow we are to take a test in geometry so me thinks I'll study and iron today. How's that?

[from Mary]

It appears that the only times Mary Church Terrell became annoyed with her husband were over their daughters. By the time the girls were teenagers, Mrs. Terrell worried that in her absence Mary and Phyllis would bring boys into the house, and that Robert wouldn't know about it because he was at work or wouldn't care because he was so easygoing. "I am dreadfully worried about the girls," she wrote to Robert on one occasion while traveling aboard a train.

> *You do the best you can, but you are a man and you are not at home when they return from school. I am worried nearly to death. I can hardly think that I shall be absent from home another whole week speaking at Youngstown, Ohio, next Monday night. You see to it that Phyllis in particular does not walk home with boys. It will not do. Give my love to the girls and tell them to behave themselves whatever they do.*
>
> *With lots of love and kisses to you all,*
> *I am your affectionate WIFIE.*

Robert wrote his wife lighthearted letters to cheer her up when she was away from home. On September 25, 1913, he wrote to her at Oberlin: "Nogi [the dog] and I are having a good time together. He continually misses you folks, however. Nogi joins me in love to the girls and you. He says he enjoyed his bath immensely this morning." On November 14, 1913, just before Mary was to leave the girls in Oberlin and return home, Robert wrote her a letter reporting that he was recovering from a severe case of food poisoning. Still, he managed to slip in a zany story about a man who killed himself because he was curious to find out if he had an immortal soul. Perhaps this tale distracted his wife from her concerns that the girls would land in trouble once she left. But we can imagine her reaction when Phyllis wrote twelve days later saying she was going on a Thanksgiving hike with some boys.

Something else troubled Mary Church Terrell. Since her youth she had yearned to be a writer. True, she had published many articles, but her dream was to write a book—especially a book of fiction. From time to time she wrote short stories, producing enough of them to fill a book. Bearing such titles as "The Mother Who Stayed at Home" and "Jane, the Cook, Scores One," most of her stories were rejected numerous times. Her sole success was "Venus and the Night Doctors," published in the *Washington Post*.

Often in her diaries she bemoaned her lack of success as a writer. Her explanation was that her roles as a wife, mother, housekeeper, public speaker, and clubwoman were so demanding that she lacked the time and energy to write. "I have done so little this year," she confessed to her diary on December 31, 1905—New Year's Eve. "I want to write but everything seems to prevent me from doing so. I hope this time next year I shall have accomplished something in that line."

Mrs. Terrell's diary entry relates that she took her daughters to the White House to see the president.

But year after year nothing changed. On March 16, 1908, she wrote: "I am caught in a vice of domestic duties which must be done by somebody and there is no somebody but myself to do it. I enjoy it but I have time for nothing else." The next day, March 17, she complained: "Rushed around to see about the sewing. It takes all my time and strength and I shall be glad when it is over."

Some of her bitterest comments came in 1909. On her forty-sixth birthday, September 23, she wrote: "This is my birthday. I have had less energy than I have had in a long time. For at least 15 years I have wanted to write a book and I seem further away from accomplishing this dream of my heart than I ever was. I am simply surrounded by cares and duties which I must perform. I hope I shall be able to devote some of my time and strength to literary work before I die." Two months later she complained: "House-keeping is a regular [tomb] in which a woman who wants to accomplish something buries her talent and time." And on December 13 she lamented: "I do not even think about anything but household matters. Writing is entirely out of the question."

As late as 1943, when she was eighty, Mrs. Terrell confessed in an article for *Negro Digest* that she greatly regretted not succeeding as a story writer. Her regrets were both for personal reasons and because she thought that racial issues could be presented better "through the medium of the short story than in any other way."

Her last statement has been proved true. Many black authors, from Richard Wright to Alice Walker, have shed light on racial matters through their stories. Perhaps Mrs. Terrell would have written better stories had she found more time to work on her fiction. But the main reason her stories didn't do well was that they were preachy and not very original. Mary Church Terrell was a superb organizer and leader, but not an outstanding fiction writer.

A person as high-strung and frustrated as Mary Church Terrell needed to let off steam. She relaxed through physical activity and games. In her forties she went back to playing tennis, which she had enjoyed in college. Typically, she couldn't just have fun but felt compelled to evaluate her progress. On August 15, 1908, she reported in her diary: "Played tennis a

The Terrells' vacation home was at Highland Beach, Maryland.

good deal. Am improving but there is a great deal of room for it." She and Robert attended baseball and football games. On May 6, 1905, she wrote: "Went to the base ball game with Hubby—had a fine time." They went to see the Washington Senators, a major league team that lost a heartbreaker to the Philadelphia Athletics, 2–1, that day. Besides serving as a municipal judge, Robert Terrell taught in Howard University's law school. In the fall the Terrells attended the Howard football games and sometimes helped at the dances and other social events held at the times of big games.

Mrs. Terrell adored dancing, boasting in her autobiography that at age seventy she could "dance as long and as well as I ever did." She also loved swimming, and jumped in the water at every opportunity. Her favorite game was whist—a card game that was the forerunner of bridge. We know that she belonged to the Matrons' Whist Club, because the noted historian Carter G. Woodson sent her a letter in care of that group. Her other favorite pastimes included hiking, which on one occasion nearly ended in disaster.

Almost every summer Mary and Robert—or just Mary if her husband couldn't get away—took their daughters on a vacation. When young Mary was about twelve and Phyllis around eight years old, the family visited Harpers Ferry, West Virginia, where they lodged at a black school called Storer College. One day Mrs. Terrell agreed to lead a group of girls on a hike up a nearby mountain. She insisted that the younger girls, including Phyllis, remain in the dormitory. Then she set out with Mary and some other girls.

A difficult climb brought them to the top of the mountain. When they started back, several girls insisted that they knew another route down. Against her better judgment Mrs. Terrell agreed to try this different path. They were partway down when the path suddenly ended. Below them

Mary Church Terrell's daughter, Mary Louise Church, relaxing on the beach.

was a sheer drop. Had it been earlier, they could have retraced their steps up the mountain and searched for their original path, but it was growing dark. Looking around that they found a narrow path down which they could descend, only it was so steep that they had to slide on their stomachs, grasping the edge to keep from tumbling over the side. One by one the girls shinnied down the narrow path, followed by Mrs. Terrell. They all made it safely down, reaching the dormitory when it was completely dark.

A worrier herself, Mary Church Terrell realized she had been incredibly foolish to take the girls down an unknown mountain path. "Several of the mothers were on the verge of hysterics" by the time their daughters returned, Terrell wrote of this frightening incident. "Since then I have never taken other women's children any place [from which] I was not sure I could return them safe and sound to their homes."

There was one other sport that Mrs. Terrell liked. Oddly enough, she was a boxing fan. At times she used boxing terms to describe herself. Writing from Chicago on November 24, 1900, she informed her husband that she had been suffering from a terrible toothache. But, she told him, "though somewhat disfigured as to my face, I am still in the ring," meaning she hadn't let it interfere with her business. In the 1930s Mrs. Terrell followed the career of a young boxer named Joe Louis and wrote him a fan letter. The "Brown Bomber" wrote back to her, graciously saying, "I shall always bend my efforts toward retaining the respect you and others have shown."

When she referred to being "still in the ring" and when she wrote to Joe Louis, Mrs. Terrell couldn't have dreamed that many years later, at the age of almost ninety, she would fight the battle of her life.

Café in Durham, North Carolina, with WHITE *and* COLORED *entrances.*

A "Meddler"

In August of 1905 Mary Church Terrell's article "The Mission of Meddlers" appeared in *Voice of the Negro*. Her theory was that civilization advanced when people refused to accept the way things were and meddled or tried to make changes. She wrote:

> *In the United States there is a need of meddlers today—active, insistent, and fearless meddlers who will spend their time investigating institutions, customs, and laws whose effect upon the citizens of any color or class is depressing or bad. . . . Among the people of no country or race is there [more] urgent need of meddlers than among the dark-skinned citizens of the United States. . . . Meddlers, more meddlers let us have . . . those who dare ask prejudiced bigots by what right they humiliate and harass their fellowmen simply on account of a difference in color or race. . . .*

At the time this article was published, forty–nine–year–old Booker T. Washington was still an important black leader. However, his theory that blacks should gradually earn a place in white society was under fire from a new generation, who believed that blacks should demand their rights as citizens. In 1903 historian W. E. B. Du Bois attacked Washington in *The Souls of Black Folk*, a landmark book celebrating black culture. Meanwhile,

Ida B. Wells was still demanding an end to lynching. Mrs. Terrell's "Meddlers" article may have been her way of saying that her sympathies were shifting toward the more militant black leaders. Although not nearly as much as she became in her old age, Mary Church Terrell turned into a bit of a "meddler" in the early 1900s.

Her first meddling involved what was called the "Brownsville Riot." In the summer of 1906 a large number of black soldiers were stationed at Fort Brown near Brownsville, Texas. Some white townspeople insulted and abused the black soldiers on the streets. On an August night in 1906 shooting broke out in Brownsville, resulting in one death and the wounding of a police lieutenant. With little investigation the government blamed the black soldiers for the shooting. All the black soldiers in three companies of troops—nearly two hundred men—were discharged "without honor" from the army. This was done despite the fact that most of the men had spotless records and there was no proof that any of them had taken part in the incident. Even if the black soldiers had been involved, probably no more than a few of them had had anything to do with the shooting, so dismissing all of them from the army was clearly unfair.

Mary Church Terrell was outraged that all the black soldiers had been blamed without evidence. She wrote articles about it. In November of 1906 she visited the Department of War in the nation's capital and asked to see William Howard Taft, President Theodore Roosevelt's secretary of war.

Mrs. Terrell sat in the waiting room hour after hour until Mr. Taft's aide finally came up to her and asked, "Why do you want to see the secretary of war?"

"I want to say a few words to Secretary Taft about the colored soldiers who have just been dismissed," Mrs. Terrell answered.

The assistant disappeared for a few minutes. Upon his return he said, "Secretary Taft is too busy to see you and he doubts that he can see you anytime today."

"I'll wait here just the same," Mrs. Terrell said firmly. "I have already been here several hours and I might as well remain longer."

Mrs. Terrell didn't budge from her chair. A good hour later the secretary of war sent word that he would see her. As soon as she entered his office, Mrs. Terrell said, "I have come to see you about the colored soldiers who have been dismissed without honor in Brownsville, Texas."

"What do you want me to do about it?" inquired Mr. Taft. "President Roosevelt has already dismissed them, and he has gone to Panama. There is nothing I can do."

"All I want you to do, Mr. Secretary," said Mrs. Terrell, "is to suspend the order dismissing the soldiers without honor, until an investigation can be made."

A giant of a man at nearly three hundred pounds, Secretary of War Taft stared in disbelief at the middle-aged black woman before him. "*All* you want me to do," he thundered, "is suspend an order issued by the president of the United States during his absence from the country!"

Mrs. Terrell pleaded for the soldiers, saying that it was unjust to blame them all for something that might have involved a few or even none of them. Taft, who in 1909 would follow Theodore Roosevelt as president and who would later serve as chief justice of the United States Supreme Court, was known for his fairness. He listened to Mary Church Terrell and agreed with much of what she said. Shortly after her departure Mr. Taft sent a telegram to President Roosevelt. He was withholding the presidential order to dismiss the black soldiers from the army until they discussed it together, the secretary of war informed Roosevelt.

Across the nation newspaper headlines announced that Mary Church Terrell had convinced the secretary of war to suspend the president's order to dismiss the black troops. The *Washington Evening Star* reported: "Mrs. Terrell stated her case with precision and effect, pleading that the colored troops be given another opportunity to defend themselves and asserting that they had not yet had their side of the case properly presented."

After President Roosevelt returned from Panama in late November, Mrs. Terrell went to see him, but he had made up his mind and carried out his decision to oust the black soldiers from the army. Not until 1972 did the United States Army admit that the Brownsville soldiers had

President Theodore Roosevelt appointed Robert Terrell as a judge, but his handling of the Brownsville affair disappointed Mrs. Terrell.

suffered a "gross injustice" and remove the "discharges without honor" from their records. After sixty-six years nearly all the soldiers had died, but at least their descendants had the satisfaction of seeing their loved ones' reputations restored.

Events like the Brownsville affair convinced many people that African Americans needed an organization to fight for their rights. On February 12, 1909—the one hundredth anniversary of President Abraham Lincoln's birth—a group of black and white leaders from around the country began the National Association for the Advancement of Colored People. The NAACP's founders included Mary Church Terrell, Ida B. Wells, and W. E. B. Du Bois. Its goals included fighting segregation and lynching and securing black people's voting rights. Du Bois became editor of *The Crisis.* This NAACP magazine was aptly named, for black Americans were suffering from poverty and injustice in crisis proportions.

Today the NAACP is generally viewed as a conservative organization. But early on it was seen as a rather militant group opposed to Booker T. Washington's gradualist ideas. Having boosted Robert Terrell's appointment as municipal judge, Washington was angry that Judge Terrell's wife had helped form the NAACP. "Of course I am not seeking to control anyone's activities, but I simply want to know where we stand," Washington wrote to Robert Terrell shortly after the founding of the NAACP. However, Washington soon accepted the fact that Mary was moving away from his way of thinking. He held no grudges against the Terrells, and even asked Robert to make an upcoming graduation speech at Tuskegee Institute.

Mary Church Terrell remained active in the NAACP for many years. In 1916 she attended the Amenia Conference. Held on the estate of NAACP official Joel Spingarn in Amenia, New York, the conference brought

The Amenia Conference of 1916; Mary Church Terrell appears to be the third person from the left in the middle row.

together white and black leaders to discuss ways to improve race relations. Three years later, in 1919, Mrs. Terrell became vice president of the NAACP branch in the nation's capital.

By the early 1900s Mary Church Terrell was involved in other social issues. She had become a suffragist—a person who fought for the right of women to vote. The issues of women being denied the vote and blacks being deprived of their civil rights were closely tied. People who worked for one cause often worked for the other. Mary Church Terrell and famed suffragist Susan B. Anthony had met in 1898 at a women's voting rights convention in Washington, D.C., and remained friends until Miss Anthony died in March of 1906. Susan B. Anthony once arranged for Mrs. Terrell to speak in Rochester, New York, and stay in her home there. Years later the National Woman's Party, formed by suffragist Alice Paul in 1913, staged marches in front of the White House. Mrs. Terrell often joined the pickets, sometimes bringing her daughter Phyllis along.

Susan B. Anthony.

Mary Church Terrell also wrote articles about women's right to vote. Her article "The Justice of Woman Suffrage" appeared in *The Crisis* in September of 1912. It was "unjust to withhold from one-half of the human race rights and privileges freely accorded the other half," she wrote. Thanks to Susan B. Anthony, Alice Paul, Mary Church Terrell, and thousands of others, American women finally won the right to vote with the Nineteenth Amendment in 1920. In the South, however, black women and men would not be allowed to vote, despite U.S. laws, for many more years.

The quest for world peace was another cause that attracted Mrs. Terrell. The 1800s had been a century of wars and more wars around the world. By the early 1900s it was apparent that deadlier wars than ever before might occur. Nations were building powerful armies, navies, and weapons. The Wright brothers made the first airplane flight in 1903, and while most people saw no practical use for this invention, some visionaries predicted that airplanes might one day be used to drop bombs.

Women in many lands felt that if they had their fair share of power, they would do better than men at preventing war and improving life for all people. In 1904 women from around the world gathered at the International Congress of Women in Berlin, Germany, to discuss issues of common interest. Mrs. Terrell was invited to speak at the Congress, and she very much wanted to go, but at that time she and Robert were having money problems. She asked her father for three hundred dollars, which he promptly sent. She sailed for Europe in the spring of 1904, arriving in Berlin in early June.

Mrs. Terrell took the stage on Monday, June 13, 1904. That evening she gave her speech "The Progress of Colored Women." She presented it differently than she did on the lecture circuit in her home country, however. Instead of just in English, she also delivered her speech in German and French.

The audience went wild. Mrs. Terrell was "the hit of the congress on the part of the American delegates," reported the *Washington Post*. The delegates, many of whom knew German or French but not English, appreciated her ability to speak their languages and her thoughtfulness in doing so.

Unfortunately, the war that many people had feared broke out in 1914 and lasted four years. Called the Great War (known today as World War I), it involved about thirty nations and claimed the most lives of any war up to that time. Of the nearly five million Americans in uniform, about 370,000 were African Americans who served in segregated, all–black units. In all, ten million soldiers died in this war and twenty–one million were wounded.

After the Great War ended in 1918, a number of groups held peace conferences in the hope of preventing such conflicts in the future. In the spring of 1919 the International Congress of Women for Permanent Peace met in Zurich, Switzerland. Mrs. Terrell was selected as a delegate to this conference. She sailed from New York with other American delegates in

Woman suffrage demonstration in Washington, D.C., in 1913.

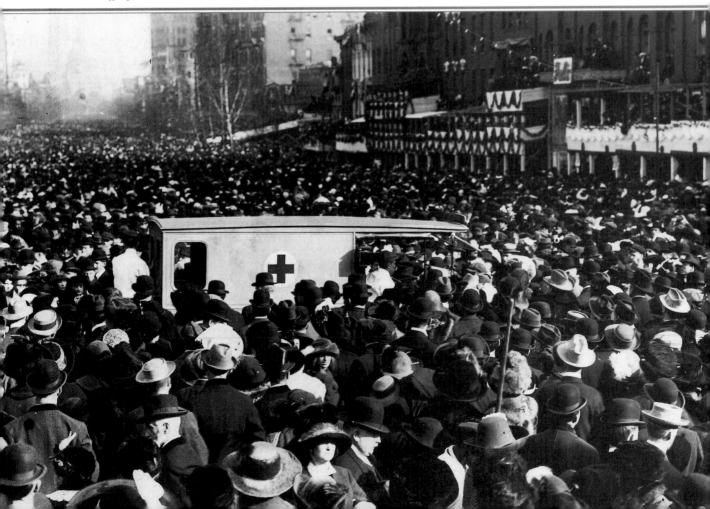

Mary Church Terrell
in middle age.

April. One of her companions was Jane Addams, the famous social worker from Chicago. Also traveling to the conference with Terrell was Jeannette Rankin of Montana, who in 1916—four years before women received the vote nationally—had become the first woman elected to the U.S. Congress.

The conference was held in Zurich in mid-May of 1919. One of the greatest moments of Mary Church Terrell's life came on Thursday, May 15, when she spoke in front of three thousand people.

"You may talk about permanent peace till doomsday," she said, "but the world will never have it till the dark races are given a square deal." Again speaking in German, as she had fifteen years earlier, she said that many white people were prejudiced not only against blacks but also against Asians and other nonwhites. She offered a stirring resolution to the convention: "We believe no human being should be deprived of an education, prevented from earning a living, debarred from any legitimate pursuit in which he wishes to engage, or be subjected to humiliation of various kinds on account of race, color, or creed." The convention approved Mrs. Terrell's resolution unanimously.

She was so thrilled by the conference that the day after it ended, she wrote a very long letter to Robert describing what had occurred. The following is just a portion:

> *Zurich*
> *Sunday, May 18, 1919*

> *My dear Husband:*
> *The Congress is over and this very rainy Sunday morning in Zurich is the first second I have been able to snatch to tell you about the marvellous impression my address made upon the audience which filled the largest Church in the City. There were nearly 3,000 people present. [It was] the greatest night of my life. There were six speakers on the program and I was the last!!! I presented my resolution, which was passed without a single dissenting vote!!! The audience went wild when I finished. There went up such an outburst, such a storm of applause, as I have not heard since I spoke in Berlin fifteen years ago!!! Among other things I said the black men who went from the United States [to fight in the war] fought for a freedom which they do not possess themselves. You know I am a harsh critic of myself, I am rarely satisfied in my heart with what I do. Well, I am perfectly happy this time over what I did. If I die tonight, I feel that after the work accomplished for a persecuted race, Thursday night, May 15, I will not have lived in vain. If I live one hun-*

dred years, I will never do more real work than I did Thursday night, May 15 in St. Peter's Cathedral. Be sure to read [this letter] to the family. Make each one listen, whether he wants to or not. Please save [this letter] for me till I get home. I sail for home June 23 on the Noordam, the same steamer I came over on.

Lots of love,
Mollie

Mary Church Terrell *did* live nearly one hundred years, but her other prediction was wrong. This was *not* the most important work she would ever do.

Mary's father, Robert Church, in later life.

"I Intend Never to Grow Old"

The years from 1910 to the early 1920s may have been the busiest of Mary Church Terrell's life. During that period she raised her daughters, lectured often, and was active in a remarkable number of organizations. Her personal papers reveal that between 1910 and 1922 she was associated with at least twenty-nine groups, in many cases regularly attending their meetings.

Meanwhile, there were changes, some of them unpleasant, in Mary Church Terrell's personal life. She and her husband had serious money problems in the early 1900s. Judge Terrell was involved with the Capital Savings Bank, a savings institution that ran into difficulty. He was forced to borrow money repeatedly from his father-in-law. "You have always been so ready to help me and you have done so much for me already," he wrote to Robert Church on April 23, 1902, referring to "the debt I already owe you." In this letter, Robert Terrell asked his father-in-law for another two thousand dollars—the equivalent of about forty thousand dollars today. Robert Church, who would do anything for his daughter and her family, sent the money.

Mary's parents both died around the same time. Her mother died in 1911. Her father died, following a brief illness, on August 29, 1912, at the age of seventy-three. Mary had been close to Robert Church and took the loss hard. His death also set off a storm of legal squabbles.

Despite his reputation as the South's first black millionaire, Church left an estate worth much less than a million dollars. His wife, Anna Wright Church, later claimed that he had left only fifteen hundred dollars in cash, all of which went for funeral expenses and bills. His holdings, however, included a vast amount of real estate. Robert Reed Church's will, dated January 14, 1911, left Anna the mansion at 384 South Lauderdale Street plus about forty buildings and lots in Memphis and a 138-acre farm. Except for a watch and chain for Robert Jr., Church didn't leave anything to his two children by his wife Anna. Still, Robert Jr. and Annette would someday be wealthy, for all the property left to Anna was to go to them after her death.

Robert Church did not forget Thomas and Mary, his children by his previous wife, Louisa. He left them, "share and share alike," approximately forty houses and twenty-three plots of land he had owned. It is impossible to calculate how much this real estate was worth then or what its value would be today, but her inheritance did not make Mary Church Terrell rich. We know this because she had to work during her later years and often paid her bills late. Advertisements in Memphis newspapers of 1912 reveal that a typical house and lot in a black neighborhood of Memphis could be bought for several hundred dollars, so forty houses and twenty-three plots of land had far less value than they would today.

There was another complication with her father's will. Robert Church, who had done so many remarkable deeds in life, provided a final surprise. Before the Civil War, slave marriages had been common. A slave couple decided to marry because they were in love, or because they were ordered to marry by an owner who wanted some valuable slave children. Slave couples weren't allowed to have a legal ceremony with a minister and a marriage license. They merely agreed to be man and wife in front of relatives and friends.

In 1857, at the age of eighteen, Robert Church had been married in a slave wedding to a woman named Margaret Pico. Robert and Margaret were soon separated, but not before she had given birth to a daughter named Laura. After Robert Church died in 1912, Laura Church Napier

Mary Church Terrell (seated) at the time of her father's death; at right is her half-sister Annette Church and at left is Sara Johnson Church, wife of her half-brother, Robert Jr.

sued for a part of her father's estate. She did not try to get any of the inheritance of Mary Church Terrell and her brother, Thomas. Rather, she sued Anna Wright Church, who had received the mansion at 384 South Lauderdale Street and other more valuable properties.

Anna Church successfully fought off the lawsuit in a bitter contest that went all the way to the Tennessee Supreme Court. The situation became even nastier. Anna had spent much of her savings on successfully defending her inheritance. She was left with plenty of property but little money.

About 370,000 African Americans served in World War I; by the time of the war Abraham Lincoln had been dead for many years, but this poster shows him proudly watching some of the country's black troops.

Apparently feeling that her children should bear some of the burden since they would one day inherit the estate, in about 1917 Anna Church instituted a lawsuit against her son and daughter, Robert Jr. and Annette. To her credit, Mary Church Terrell stayed on friendly terms with this branch of her father's family—at least for the time being.

By April 1917, when the United States entered World War I, Mrs. Terrell's lecturing had tapered off. She was tired of traveling and, besides, the public was more interested in the war than in what she had to say about racial problems. The federal government in Washington needed clerks, and the Terrells needed a boost in their income. Mary passed the test to be a typist and filled out an application for the job, stating that she could speak, read, and write German and French. In the part of the questionnaire that asked about her race, she wrote "American," for she knew many qualified black people who had been turned down because of their color. Late one night she received a telegram asking her to report to the office of a General Crozier.

The next morning, when a secretary led her into the general's office, Mrs. Terrell found him studying her application. "You have had very fine training indeed," said General Crozier. "We need the services of those who understand German and French," he added, for France was an ally of the United States in the war, while Germany was an enemy. But then the general looked at her closely for the first time. She saw his expression change as he suddenly realized that she was a light-skinned black woman.

"I see that you have taught in a high school here," he said. "Which one was it?"

"I taught in the M Street High School," Mrs. Terrell answered.

Everyone in Washington knew that this school was for black students and teachers. The general pushed her application aside.

"Mrs. Terrell," he inquired, "have you ever had any office experience?"

She had already explained on her application that she hadn't, Mary Church Terrell answered, but the general, who moments before had been so eager to hire her, used this as an excuse to reject her. "Good morning," he said, showing her to the door.

Shortly after this disappointment, she applied to a government office called the War Risk Insurance Bureau and was hired as a clerk. Her job was to process records of soldiers who were physically ill or mentally disturbed. The person who hired her assumed she was dark-skinned but white, and placed her in a room with white women. The officials in charge of the office soon realized that a black woman was in their midst. Some of them, especially a white physician from the South, objected. They decided to get rid of her by saying she hadn't done her job correctly. In mid-October of 1917, after two months in the office, Mrs. Terrell received a letter stating: "You have made numerous mistakes, and when these were called to your attention you caused considerable disturbance and tended to deny responsibility. You do not want to or cannot understand the requests of your superiors in the matter of properly performing duties assigned to you."

None of this was true. Why was a highly educated woman who met with presidents and had spoken to huge audiences being accused of doing a simple job improperly? The charges had been concocted to get rid of her because she was black, Mrs. Terrell knew. She wanted to fight back, but the controversy might hurt her husband's career as a Municipal Court judge. She swallowed her pride and was fired from the War Risk Insurance Bureau.

Next she found a job at the Census Bureau. At first the white and black clerks worked in the same room, but soon the black employees were moved to separate quarters and told that they couldn't use the same bathroom as the white clerks. This time Mrs. Terrell did not remain quiet. She complained about the segregated facilities and quit in protest.

After the war ended in November 1918, she landed another government job, this time with the War Camp Community Service. She was to help set up recreational centers for black people around the country, especially black soldiers returning from Europe. Traveling to Illinois, Alabama, Mississippi, Tennessee, Georgia, Florida, Virginia, and New York, she helped establish numerous community centers. She continued at this job for a few months before leaving for the women's peace convention in Zurich, Switzerland, in the spring of 1919.

The worst blow of her life occurred two years later. In 1921 her husband suffered a severe stroke. Robert Terrell had to resign his position as a judge and was a housebound invalid for the last four and a half years of his life. Mary gave up many of her activities to care for him. Five days before Christmas of 1925, Robert died at the age of sixty-eight. He had been the love of her life, her companion for thirty-four years, the person who could calm her worries with a funny story, and one of the two men—the other being her father—she most admired.

At the time of her husband's death, Mary Church Terrell was sixty-two years old. Her daughters, Mary and Phyllis, were now adults and, despite her fears, had turned out well. Both became teachers in the Washington public schools and got married—Phyllis to a school principal and Mary to a physician named Leon Tancil. Although not rich, Mrs. Terrell had her Washington home, a vacation house at Highland Beach on Chesapeake Bay near Annapolis, Maryland, and a small income from the property her father had left her. Looking back on her life, she felt proud of her achievements: first black woman on the Washington Board of Education, first president of the NACW, a founder of the NAACP, and one of the most popular lecturers of her era. It was time to fulfill her dream, she decided. She would write a book—only instead of fiction it would be the true story of her life.

Mary Church Terrell began writing her autobiography in early 1927, when she was sixty-three. She worked steadily, writing the first draft by hand, sometimes on the backs of letters or advertisements if no other paper was handy. She saved every page of every version she wrote, and as a result the various drafts of the book comprise nearly seventeen hundred pages and occupy twenty-three folders in the Mary Church Terrell Papers at the Library of Congress. Several times she ripped up a page but then gathered the pieces and taped them together to save them for posterity.

While working on this giant project, she still did some civil rights work and public speaking. For example, her diary entry for Valentine's Day of 1927 describes her meeting that day with President Calvin Coolidge:

A COLORED drinking fountain in North Carolina, as seen in 1938.

*Went to White House and spoke about segregation, lynching,
the imprisoned soldiers and I was presented to the President.*

But her autobiography became her consuming passion. On days
when the project went well, she was happy. Setbacks with the book
depressed her. On February 27, 1935, after finishing a draft, she wrote in
her diary: "Finished manuscript at last—Gott sei Dank!" Those last three
words mean "Thank God!" in German. She celebrated by going to see the
movie *David Copperfield*. But the next day, when she went to show her
manuscript to the mystery writer Mary Roberts Rinehart, she was
crushed to find that the famous author had forgotten their appointment
and wasn't there. "Bitter, Bitter Disappointment!" she began her diary
entry for February 28, 1935:

I took my manuscript to Mrs. Rinehart today and when I reached her residence she had gone. Her secretary told me she was going to live in New York. He said it was all done suddenly. If I had only known! Just one week too late! If I could only have talked with her about my manuscript and have asked her some questions while she was here.

Even before her final version was complete, she began sending the manuscript to publishers. Each rejection was painful. On Friday, April 12, 1935, she wrote in her diary: "I am perfectly wretched, miserable because my manuscript has been rejected."

With her husband gone, one of the few people who could lift her spirits after a writing disappointment was her brother. Thomas had become a lawyer in New York City and was also an author. He shared their mother's interest in birds and drawing. His best-known work was *The Roller*, a book he wrote and illustrated about the care and training of a kind of singing canary.

"Now in reference to your book, by no means allow yourself to become discouraged nor disheartened," Thomas Church wrote in one letter. He then told his sister about a much-rejected playwright who eventually sold her work and became a millionaire.

Mollie kept revising, year after year. Finally, after eleven years, she typed up the approximately four-hundred-page final manuscript. She considered possible titles: *A Colored Woman in the Great White World*, *The Confessions of a Colored Woman*, and *A Mighty Rocky Road*. Her final choice was *A Colored Woman in a White World*. She was seventy-five years old when she completed her manuscript in 1938.

Mary Church Terrell sent out her autobiography with high hopes, thinking now that it was finished, she would have a better chance of selling it. Publisher after publisher rejected her manuscript. She even hand-delivered it to editors in New York City, but that didn't help. Her closest brush with success came in January of 1940, when a major publisher rejected her manuscript after many months with the explanation: "We admire your achievement but our people doubt whether publication could be satisfactorily profitable to both you and to us."

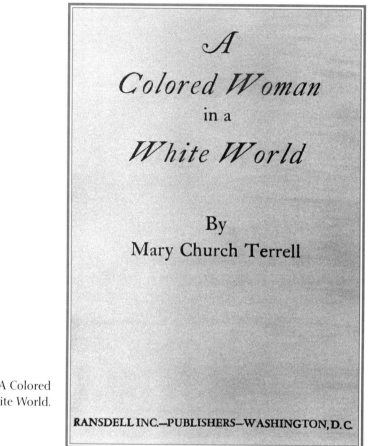

Title page of A Colored Woman in a White World.

Having her autobiography turned down dozens of times after eleven years of work devastated Mrs. Terrell, who felt that her life as well as her writing had been rejected. She was convinced that no major publisher would take her book because white people, who made up about ninety percent of the population, did not want to read about a black person's life. But *Narrative of the Life of Frederick Douglass,* Booker T. Washington's *Up From Slavery,* and other autobiographies by black people had been successful. Perhaps the reason for all the rejections was that she had omitted many important details of her life, such as why her mother attempted suicide, or why she and her husband adopted Mary.

In 1940 Mrs. Terrell turned to an author's last resort—a vanity press. Major publishers pay authors for the right to print their books. With a vanity press it works the opposite way: The author pays the publisher. The Ransdell Company, a vanity press in Washington, D.C., said that for $1,566.80 it would produce one thousand copies of her book, which she could then try to sell on her own. The amount Ransdell wanted was equal to about $20,000 in today's money, which was difficult for Mrs. Terrell to scrape together. But she was eager to have her book published, so she made the deal.

A Colored Woman in a White World came out in the fall of 1940. Mrs. Terrell sent free copies to magazines and newspapers, which generally reviewed the book favorably, and to major publishers, in the hope that one of them would like it enough to reprint it. The book appeared at an inopportune time, however. The nation had turned its attention to World War II (1939–1945), which it entered in 1941 and which would be the deadliest war ever fought. Over the course of about eight years, Mrs. Terrell sold only a few hundred copies of her book at $2.50 apiece. She probably broke even or perhaps lost money on the venture. What disturbed her most was that she had hoped her autobiography would inspire young people. Instead, she remained a little-known figure from the distant past to the new generation. As late as February of 1954, when she was ninety years old, Mary Church Terrell was still trying without success to convince a major publisher to reissue her book.

"I do not feel old. I intend never to grow old," Mrs. Terrell had written in "Carrying On," her book's final chapter:

> *My friends are constantly telling me that I must put the soft pedal on some of my activities and I try to take their advice. But I cannot. I am just not built that way. I can walk faster and farther than either one of my daughters without feeling it. And I have greater power of endurance than either one of them has. I can dance as long and as well as I ever did, although I get very few chances to do so.*

Mary Church Terrell never became a grandmother, for neither Phyllis nor Mary had children. Although she barely mentioned it in her autobiography, and the facts must be assembled from scattered clues, there was another addition to her family in 1937.

Her brother, Thomas, had two children. First came Mary Louise, born to an unknown mother around 1894 and adopted by Mary Church Terrell and her husband around 1900. Many years later Thomas married a white woman named Anna Tanal and with her had a son named Thomas Jr., who was born in 1927. Mrs. Terrell and her nephew were close, often visiting each other and exchanging holiday cards. When he was eight and just learning to type, Thomas Jr. sent her this note, which she saved:

New York City
Nov. 9 1935

Dear aunt:
How are you feeling i hope you are alright. My father bought me some books King Arthur and his knights, Robinson Crusoe, Alice in Wonderland. I said thank you and my father bought me Gullivers Travels please excuse my mistakes and errors

YOUR NEPHEW
Thomas church

PS. I also have the book Treasure Island and Pinnocchio

your nephew
Thomas A. Church

Mary Church Terrell's adopted daughter, Mary Tancil, and her husband had settled in Chicago. By about 1936 Mrs. Terrell's brother, Thomas, was in poor health and moved to Chicago to live with his daughter. Early in 1937, Thomas Church died. Apparently his savings had been wiped out by the hard times known as the Great Depression, for when Mary Church Terrell got to Chicago, she learned she would have to pay for her brother's funeral. Her nephew, Thomas Jr., was also in Chicago at this time. Mrs. Terrell made a plan. Nearly forty years earlier she had adopted her brother's daughter, Mary. Now she and that adopted daughter decided that, between them, they would raise Thomas Jr.

Two other people wanted the child, though. One was Thomas Jr.'s mother, who had been hospitalized for two years with a nervous ailment. The other was Mrs. Terrell's half-brother, Robert Church Jr., who had also come to Chicago to be with the family. A prominent banker and politician, Robert Church Jr. had one child, a daughter. While the family was gathered in Chicago, Robert Church Jr. told Mary Church Terrell that he planned to adopt his nephew, Thomas Jr., and raise him in Memphis as his son.

On Friday, March 5, 1937, while still in Chicago, Mrs. Terrell returned to her daughter Mary's home to find her half-brother waiting for her. Robert Church Jr. had learned of Mary Church Terrell's plans for Thomas Jr., and he was angry.

"I told you I would keep Thomas," said Robert Jr., according to a description of the scene Mrs. Terrell wrote in her diary.

Trying to avoid a fight with her half-brother, she answered, "I didn't think you meant it."

"I don't say what I don't mean!" declared Robert Jr., adding that he wasn't going to let either Mary Church Terrell or Mary Tancil raise the boy. "Nobody but a Church heir shall keep him," said Robert Jr., referring to the fact that he and his sister, Annette, had inherited the bulk of their father's estate after Anna Church's death in 1928.

Suddenly, Mrs. Terrell grew very angry. She threatened to hire a lawyer and said, "You are the last person in the world Brother would want to raise his son."

"I don't know that!" said Robert Church Jr., who at fifty-one was twenty-two years younger than his half-sister.

"But I do!" replied Mrs. Terrell, absolutely determined to have her way.

Mary Church Terrell hired lawyers and won, for on June 2, 1937, she wrote in her diary: "The lawsuit to keep Thomas from his white, mentally ill mother and Robert Church who tried to take the child from me cost $275." We know that Thomas Jr. lived in Chicago with his older half-sister, for when writing letters to her mother, Mary Tancil referred to the boy as part of her

Mary Church Terrell with her daughter Phyllis and Thomas Church Jr.

household. Mrs. Terrell sent her daughter money for Thomas Jr.'s upkeep. Later she helped put him through college. Like his father before him, Thomas Jr. eventually became a lawyer in New York City.

Mary Church Terrell worried as much about Thomas Jr. as she had about her two daughters. Actually, the fact that Phyllis and Mary were now in their thirties and forties changed nothing for Mrs. Terrell, who still babied and worried about them, too.

When separated from her daughters or from Thomas Jr., Mrs. Terrell couldn't rest unless they called or wrote to her. In July of 1937 she presented a speech at the World Fellowship of Faiths in London, England. Writing from London's Savoy Hotel, she did her best to make Phyllis feel guilty for not sending her a letter:

My darling Daughter:

Surely you must be ill! I have not received one line from you since I left home. I do not believe you would treat me that way unless something had happened to you. I don't know where you are. . . . Mary has written me several letters. I'll send this to Highland Beach hoping you are there. Don't fail to have a letter at the hotel for me. . . .

With lots of love and kisses,
Mother

Fifteen years later, nothing had changed. In the summer of 1952 the NACW held its convention in Los Angeles, California. Mrs. Terrell attended the convention and stayed with her daughter Mary, who had moved to Los Angeles. From her daughter's home, Mary Church Terrell wrote a letter to Phyllis describing the convention. She concluded by asking about Thomas Jr., who evidently was living in Washington at that time, and then gave her daughter step-by-step instructions about sending an airmail letter:

Where is Thomas? What is he doing? Is he sleeping at our house? I wish I did not have several things at home on my mind. I would have more peace. However, I am trying to be sensible and am reasonably successful in banishing forbidden subjects from my mind. Please reply immediately and send it Air Mail. If Fannie has no Air Mail stamps, put 2 three cent stamps on the letter and write AIR MAIL under them. I send oodles of love.

Mother

At this time Mrs. Terrell was a few weeks shy of her eighty-ninth birthday and her daughter Phyllis—whom she was telling how to mail a letter—was fifty-four!

What with the upkeep of her homes in Washington and Highland Beach, Maryland, Mrs. Terrell found herself in need of money. She worked on and off as a government clerk past the age of seventy. She may have lied about

Mary Church Terrell remained elegant as she aged.

her age in order to work longer. On her passport when she went to the women's peace conference in Zurich in 1919, Mrs. Terrell wrote that she was born on September 23, 1867, shaving four years off her age. But whether she made a habit of claiming to be younger than she was is unknown.

Despite what she had written about "never growing old," Mary Church Terrell's health began to falter in her seventies. In 1938—around the time that she completed her autobiography—she checked into the Battle Creek Sanitarium in Michigan for a week of rest. She returned there four years later for another week to calm her nerves. As she aged, she had to wear a hearing aid and be fitted for false teeth. She also became more forgetful, often not recalling where she had left her teeth or keys. Sometimes Mrs. Terrell played a game called "Can You Guess Where I've Hidden My Teeth?" with people around the house to see if *they* could figure out where she had left her false teeth. On July 14, 1935, she reported in her diary: "Lost my teeth for a while and found them in a glass of water in the kitchen where I had forgotten I had placed them." A few weeks later Mrs. Terrell made a trip to Oberlin and, upon her return, discovered that she had left the door unlocked during her absence.

Mary Church Terrell was injured in several accidents. At a time when relatively few women drove, she had her own car. Around 1927 she collided with a telephone company truck and broke her kneecap, requiring surgery. She sued the telephone company and was angry when the firm offered her just three hundred dollars to settle the case—an amount that didn't even cover her surgeon's bill. On December 22, 1927, Mrs. Terrell's lawyer sent her a letter advising her to take the money. "The fact that the dog was in the car and that in your testimony you spoke of watching the dog and conversing with the lady with you, added to the fact that your car was on the wrong side of the road when the impact occurred, convinces me that it will be almost hopeless" to collect more money, her attorney wrote.

The accident report showed that, besides not paying attention to her driving, Mary Church Terrell was speeding on a wet pavement. Somehow, Mrs. Terrell still felt that she was the innocent party. She accepted the three-hundred-dollar offer from the telephone company but didn't let the accident stop her from driving. A decade later, at the age of seventy-three, she bought a new 1937 Ford.

As she grew older, Mrs. Terrell walked with a cane. She suffered a terrible fall in the summer of 1951. On the night of August 19 she was returning to her summer home at Highland Beach after visiting a friend. At the foot of her steps she tripped and struck her head and shoulder on the ground. Blood oozed from her forehead. At first she couldn't get up. Finally, she pulled herself to her feet and made it into her house. It took her a long time to stop the bleeding, and the pains in her head and shoulder were so severe, she couldn't sleep that night. Her biggest worry, though, was that she would stain her clothes or mattress with blood. "Feared dress would be ruined with blood stains," she wrote when recounting this incident in her diary.

Neither her daughter Phyllis nor anyone else could convince Mrs. Terrell, who was approaching her eighty-eighth birthday, to see a doctor. Three days after the accident Mary Church Terrell reported in her diary: "Shoulder much better. Glad I didn't go to a doctor."

It was fortunate that she recovered so quickly, for by this time she was the central figure in one of the most important civil rights cases in United States history.

Portrait of Mary Church Terrell, painted in 1946, when she was 83 years old.

"Your Indomitable Spirit"

In later life Mary Church Terrell became more fiery in her opposition to injustice. After her husband died, she no longer had to worry about damaging his career if she spoke out. Also, she saw that the slow, cautious approach to civil rights hadn't worked.

There was yet another reason for her transformation. More than a million African Americans in the armed services had helped the United States and its allies win World War II. But after the war ended in 1945, the black veterans returned to a nation where many of them were prevented from voting and excluded from good jobs and housing. Like other black leaders, Terrell called for a "Double V." The United States had won a victory over its enemies overseas. Now it was time to win a victory over discrimination at home.

Starting in 1946 she worked harder than ever before to fight discrimination. That year she applied for admission to the Washington, D.C., branch of the American Association of University Women (AAUW). Mary Church Terrell had all the proper qualifications but one: She wasn't white. Mrs. Terrell received a letter stating, "The executive committee of the Washington Branch, AAUW, has voted not to approve your application for membership." After a three-year struggle, eighty-six-year-old Mrs. Terrell was admitted to the AAUW's Washington branch. Her victory paved the way for other black women to join the organization.

Also in 1949 Mary Church Terrell became chairwoman of the National Committee to Free Rosa Ingram and Her Sons. A poor black woman from Georgia, Rosa Ingram had been attacked by a white neighbor who may have been trying to rape her. The man chased her with a knife and a shotgun, then struck her on the head. Mrs. Ingram's sons, fifteen-year-old Wallace and thirteen-year-old Sammie Lee, heard her cries and ran to defend her. They fought off the attacker, killing him.

Despite the fact that they had acted in self-defense, Mrs. Ingram and her two sons were sentenced to die in the electric chair. The death sentences were changed to life in prison because of widespread protests, but the Ingram committee wanted the mother and sons freed. Mary Church Terrell organized demonstrations and circulated petitions to try to win the Ingrams' release. One petition was sent to President Harry S. Truman. Another, containing 100,000 signatures, went to the United Nations.

Oppressed people in various parts of the world also claimed Mrs. Terrell's attention. Her papers reveal that during the 1940s she helped groups that worked on behalf of homeless Jewish people, the people of India, and poor American sharecroppers, both black and white.

Still, her greatest deeds seemed to be in the past, which wasn't surprising considering her age. Then along came the greatest opportunity of her life.

Mrs. Terrell's hometown—Washington, D.C.—was one of America's most segregated cities. In 1946 President Truman created the President's Committee on Civil Rights. A year later this committee issued *To Secure These Rights*, a pamphlet describing civil rights abuses in America. Regarding the lack of opportunity for an African American in the nation's capital, the booklet reported:

> *With very few exceptions, he is refused service at downtown restaurants, he may not attend a downtown movie or play, and he has to go into a poorer section of the city to find a night's lodging. The Negro who decides to settle in the District must often find a home in an overcrowded, substandard area. He must often take a job below the level of his ability. He must*

Late in life Mrs. Terrell received honorary degrees from several colleges; little did anyone realize that her greatest deeds still lay ahead of her.

send his children to the inferior public schools set aside for Negroes and entrust his family's health to medical agencies which give inferior service. In addition, he must endure the countless daily humiliations that the system of segregation imposes upon the one-third of Washington that is Negro.

By the late 1940s black Washingtonians worked mainly at such "Negro jobs" as janitors, servants, elevator operators, and cooks. They lived mainly in segregated neighborhoods known as the capital's "black belts," which included some of the nation's worst slums. A black family that could afford to move to an upscale neighborhood might be out of luck. Section 5, Article 15 of the Washington Real Estate Board Code of Ethics for 1948 stated: "No property in a white section should ever be sold, rented, advertised, or offered to colored people."

At this time the city's African American population was growing dramatically. In 1940, 187,000 of Washington's 663,000 people—or 28 percent of the total—were African Americans. By 1950, 281,000 of Washington's 802,000 residents—or 35 percent of the total—were black.

Black babies in the nation's capital were almost twice as likely to die as white infants, and their mothers were six times as likely to die as white mothers. Black toddlers couldn't use swings and teeter-totters in whites-only parks. As a result of the Jim Crow school system, "white" junior highs had almost two thousand empty seats, while thousands of black students could attend school only part-time because of overcrowding in the "colored" schools. A black student wanting to attend college might enroll in the mainly black Howard University, or in Catholic University, which by the late 1940s had lifted its color barrier. But the capital city's prestigious George Washington University and Georgetown University admitted no blacks, and American University allowed African Americans into only one off-campus program.

Jim Crow created many outrageous situations. In the fall of 1947 Washington's Junior Chamber of Commerce held a public speaking competition. The finals of the contest were to take place in a public school auditorium, but some people objected to having black and white students on the same stage, so the contest did not go on as planned. The subject of the speeches was to be the Bill of Rights, which insures Americans of such basic rights as freedom of speech.

Marbles was a popular children's game in the 1940s. The nation's capital held *two* marbles tournaments—one for the city's white youngsters and the other for its colored children. But Washington could send only one champion to the national marbles tournament. Instead of holding a playoff between the two winners, the city automatically selected the white champion to represent Washington in the national tournament. The colored champion was automatically named runner-up for the city. This was done to keep black and white children from playing marbles together—and to prevent the possibility of a black child winning the city and national titles.

Washington, D.C., had a dog cemetery. But in the 1940s only animals belonging to white people could be buried there. Dogs whose owners were black were excluded. When asked about it, the owner of the pet cemetery joked that although the dogs wouldn't care, he believed his white customers would.

"Washington—Disgrace to the Nation," an article by Howard Whitman in the February 1950 *Woman's Home Companion*, described black people being turned away from downtown restaurants and theaters. In one case a group of black people, including some soldiers, tried to see a film called *Home of the Brave*. DANGER DRAWS NO COLOR LINE! proclaimed posters outside the theater. But the theater manager phoned the police, who made sure that no black people got into the movie. *Home of the Brave* is a classic movie about a black soldier suffering from discrimination.

It was common knowledge among black Washingtonians that, except for government cafeterias and a few other places, they couldn't eat in downtown restaurants. They also knew that they were not allowed in many Washington hotels. But these restrictions often came as a shock to visitors from other parts of the nation or from foreign lands. For example, many schools planned trips to the nation's capital. The black students couldn't always eat in the same restaurants or stay in the same hotels as the white students. Under the headline "Race Bias in Washing-

COLORED WAITING ROOM *for bus passengers in Durham, North Carolina, in 1940 . . .*

ton Deprives 51 Youngsters of Trip to Capital," the May 14, 1948, *New York Times* described a Washington trip that had been planned for winners of a safety patrol contest from the New York City region. The trip was canceled because four black youngsters would have had to stay in a separate hotel.

Two years later, in the summer of 1950, a gathering of Boy Scouts took place in Washington, D.C. Scouting officials arranged ahead of time for meals to be served to everyone at this get-together. Nonetheless, the black Scouts were turned away from at least one cafeteria.

It should be pointed out that Washington wasn't unique. Sadly, black people in many other American cities and towns, North and South, were treated similarly to those in the U.S. capital.

Sometime between 1940 and 1943 two old, forgotten laws prohibiting discrimination in Washington, D.C., were brought to light. This important discovery took place in a library. A man named Tomlinson Todd came across the old laws while doing research at the Library of Congress in the nation's capital. Mary Church Terrell later recalled that Todd, who was her friend and neighbor and also director of the *Americans All* radio show, informed her of the old laws and often remarked: "The people of Washington should do something about this, Mrs. Terrell." News of what became known as the "lost laws" spread, and they were mentioned in a 1948 booklet, *Segregation in Washington*, published by a group in Chicago.

To understand how the laws were "lost," it helps to know that over the years the national capital has undergone several changes in its city government. For a while in the 1870s the city had a governor appointed by

. . . and a WHITE WAITING ROOM at the bus terminal in Memphis, Tennessee, in 1943.

the president as well as an elected legislative assembly. Lewis Douglass, son of Frederick Douglass, was a member of Washington's short-lived assembly. Intending to protect the rights of black Washingtonians, Lewis Douglass introduced an anti-discrimination law, which was passed on June 20, 1872. It stated, in part:

> *Any restaurant keeper, hotel keeper, or keepers of ice-cream saloons or places where soda-water is kept for sale, or keepers of barber shops and bathing houses, refusing to sell or wait upon any respectable, well-behaved person, without regard to race, color, or previous condition of servitude . . . in the same room, and at the same prices as other well-behaved and respectable persons are served, shall be deemed guilty of a misdemeanor, and upon conviction in a court having jurisdiction, shall be fined $100, and shall forfeit his or her license . . . until a period of one year shall have elapsed.*

Poor black neighborhood in Washington, D.C., with a U.S. government building in the background; this picture appeared in the 1948 booklet Segregation in Washington.

Graphic from Segregation in Washington, showing how blacks suffered from discrimination in the nation's capital in the 1940s.

A second law, passed in 1873, made similar provisions to prevent discrimination in the city. But then in 1874 the U.S. Congress abolished Washington's legislative assembly. In its place Congress established a city government made up of three commissioners appointed by the nation's president. The new government never repealed the 1872 and 1873 anti-discrimination laws.

These laws were ignored, however. Restaurants, hotels, and other public gathering places excluded African Americans by custom, and nothing was done about it. The few black people who requested service were powerless and were turned away. When Washington's laws were compiled in 1901, the 1872 and 1873 anti-discrimination laws weren't even mentioned. They were also omitted in subsequent lists of the city's laws up to the 1940s. It was almost as if the laws had never existed—until Tomlinson Todd discovered them in a dusty old book at the Library of Congress.

In May 1949, just six months after the laws were discussed in *Segregation in Washington*, a group of seven Washington-area lawyers offered their opinion about the lost laws. Yes, the laws had been ignored and forgotten, said the lawyers. But they had never been repealed. In their opinion this meant that they were still in effect. Anyone who refused to serve a "respectable, well-behaved person" because of race was subject to a fine and the loss of his business license for a year.

On June 25, 1949, Mary Church Terrell and approximately twenty-five other people gathered at the Phillis Wheatley branch of the Young Women's Christian Association in Washington to discuss the lost laws. They decided to form an organization dedicated to using the old laws to fight discrimination in the U.S. capital.

Their organization was named the Coordinating Committee for the Enforcement of the D.C. Anti-Discrimination Laws, known as the Committee, or the CCEAD for short. The Committee needed a leader. Since the campaign involved a fight for black people's rights, this person should be black. He or she should be a highly "respectable" and respected person, because the lost laws contained that terminology. Most important, the group's chairperson should be an eloquent speaker and an inspiring leader. Who was better qualified than Mary Church Terrell? On September 29 the Committee's executive secretary, Annie Stein, wrote to Mrs. Terrell, asking her to be its chairman.

Annie Stein (front row, far left) did much of the day-to-day work of the CCEAD; other Committee members in this photograph include Alice Trigg (front row, second from right) and Mary Church Terrell (front row, center).

Mary Church Terrell thought of a number of reasons to say no. For one thing, she had celebrated her eighty-sixth birthday a few days earlier, on September 23. The campaign might be long and difficult, so perhaps a younger leader was needed. Moreover, all her life she had fought discrimination with words: by writing, speaking, and holding meetings. Even after becoming a "meddler," she had just used stronger words rather than taking strong action. In fact, not very many African Americans had taken a militant stand on racial issues. This campaign might involve demonstrations at restaurants and hotels, and clashes and court battles with people and organizations that favored discrimination. Was she ready to attack racism head-on?

It didn't take her long to make up her mind. Over more than half a century she had belonged to dozens of organizations, written numerous articles, and presented hundreds of speeches—and still Jim Crow was rampant. This was a chance—probably her last chance—to actually change things. Within a few days she agreed to serve as CCEAD chairman.

Under her leadership, meetings were held every week or two. From her days as NACW president she knew that there was strength in numbers. The Committee was financed through donations rather than dues, enabling poorer people to join. Eventually more than twelve hundred people, both black and white, joined the CCEAD, as did about sixty churches and more than a hundred organizations. Besides Mrs. Terrell, Committee leaders included Washington activist and labor union organizer Annie Stein; the Reverend William Jernagin, who had served as pastor of Washington's Mt. Carmel Baptist Church for thirty-seven years; the Reverend Arthur Elmes of People's Congregational Church; newspaperman Marvin Caplin; Verdie Robinson, a Washington man employed by the post office; and Alice Trigg, a Red Cross worker.

Many organizations have crumbled because of squabbles over who should receive credit for the work. Hundreds of CCEAD members, however, worked almost anonymously for their cause. For example, executive secretary Annie Stein put in many twelve-hour days sending out notices of meetings, informing people of the status of the campaign, and writing letters asking for donations. Yet few people today know about her giant contribution to the lost-laws campaign.

The Committee decided to begin with Washington restaurants that excluded black people. They would work to integrate these eating places on two fronts. First, they would wage a legal battle, arguing in court that the lost laws were still valid and must be enforced. Second, Committee members would visit restaurants that were known to discriminate and try to get them to admit black customers. That way if the courts ruled in their favor, the Committee would have a head start in actually integrating the restaurants.

Acting on their own, Mrs. Terrell knew, the Committee might have trouble convincing a court to enforce the lost laws. Their case would pack more of a wallop if Washington's city government joined their legal fight. Mrs. Terrell and other Committee leaders tried to speak with the three commissioners who governed Washington. But the commissioners wouldn't meet with them, saying that they were "studying" the lost laws and the question of whether they could be used to integrate restaurants.

THE PITTSBURGH COURIER

Bias Attacked—For refusal to serve Negroes despite an old city code saying such is illegal, Thompson's Restaurant, 725 Fourteenth Street, N. W., Washington, is the center of attack in a test case in the nation's capital, scheduled for March 31.

Thompson's Cafeteria, as shown in the Pittsburgh Courier *in 1950.*

October, November, and December passed, and still the city's commissioners and corporation counsel (lawyers) were "studying" the issue. The new year, 1950, began and nothing had changed. There were several possible reasons for this, Mrs. Terrell knew. City officials might not care much about segregation—or might even approve of it. They might be reluctant to fight the powerful Washington Restaurant Association, which favored segregation. Or they could be afraid to antagonize pro-segregation southern lawmakers in the U.S. Senate and House of Representatives.

While continuing to pressure the city commissioners and lawyers, Mrs. Terrell and her coworkers concluded that the time had come for something more than words. On January 27, 1950, the Committee chairperson and three companions, one of them white, entered Thompson's Cafeteria, where Mrs. Terrell was denied her bowl of soup and the Reverend William Jernagin and Mrs. Geneva Brown were also refused service. This action seems to have convinced city officials that Mary Church Terrell's group wasn't going to go away and must be taken seriously. A month later, on February 21, 1950, the commissioners declared that the lost laws were still in effect as far as they could tell but that they needed a second test case to bring to court.

Exactly one week later, on February 28, Mrs. Terrell visited the restaurant a second time. Again she and her two black colleagues were turned away. Armed with signed statements by Mary Church Terrell and the others who had accompanied her into Thompson's Cafeteria, the city's lawyers took the case to court.

Thompson's Cafeteria had some powerful allies. The Washington Restaurant Association, an organization representing area restaurant owners, sent a letter to thousands of eating places in Washington, D.C., Maryland, and Virginia. The *Pittsburgh Courier*, a leading black newspaper, intercepted a copy of this letter and published it:

WASHINGTON RESTAURANT ASSOCIATION
Restaurant Association Building
2003 Eye Street, N.W.
Washington 6, D.C.
"HOSPITALITY AND GOOD FOOD
FOR GOOD HEALTH"

March 13, 1950

To all Members of the Industry:
You have been advised [of] a test case to determine whether the old Acts of the Legislative Assembly of 1872 and 1873 are, at this late date, in effect in the District of Columbia. A DEFENSE FUND is absolutely necessary. One member of the Association, the John R. Thompson

Company, has been charged with a violation of the Acts, namely, that it refused to serve persons of the Negro race. A plea of Not Guilty has been entered and the case has been set for hearing in the Police Branch of the Municipal Court for the District of Columbia, Friday, March 31st, 1950. The Association has engaged [a legal] firm to defend the above case.

This [letter] is being directed not only to all local restaurants, but [also] to those in Maryland and Virginia, the theory being that they, also, may be vitally affected by the outcome of this case. It is vital that each of us defend the practices of our industry. Make your checks payable to the Washington Restaurant Defense Fund and mail today, as we must have this in by March 25, 1950.

President, Washington Restaurant Ass'n.

The *Pittsburgh Courier* also reported that the Washington Restaurant Association hoped to raise $100,000 for the legal defense of Thompson's Cafeteria. In today's money, that would be roughly $700,000.

Shortly before the trial Mrs. Terrell released a statement on behalf of the Committee. "Those who are trying to enforce the anti-discrimination laws here in Washington are rendering their country a great service," she said. "They are trying to stop it from being disgraced any longer by hotels and restaurants refusing to serve colored people in the capital of what is called the greatest democracy on earth."

The case was heard on March 31, 1950, in the Municipal Court of Judge Frank H. Myers. The commissioners accused Thompson's Cafeteria of violating the 1872 and 1873 anti-discrimination laws by refusing to serve Mary Church Terrell and her associates.

A packed courtroom listened as the lawyers argued back and forth. The old laws were "unreasonable" and were no longer in effect because they had been ignored for decades, argued Ringgold Hart, the lawyer hired by the Washington Restaurant Association to defend Thompson's Cafeteria.

"What is unreasonable about a bill that makes it possible for colored people to eat?" responded Clark King, attorney for Mrs. Terrell and her companions and the city of Washington. "It seems to me that the very concept of our Constitution is that there is no discrimination on the basis of race, creed, or color."

On it went for about three hours, Clark King insisting that discrimination was wrong, and Ringgold Hart arguing that the old laws were dead because of disuse. When the talking ended, Judge Myers retired to consider the evidence. A hundred and one days would pass before he delivered his verdict.

While awaiting the judge's decision, the CCEAD planned strategies for prodding eating places into accepting black customers. Mary Church Terrell and other Committee leaders decided to start by sending groups of two to four people to downtown restaurants, soda fountains, and lunch counters that had excluded African Americans. Some little groups would be all black; others would be composed of both black and white people. These "checkers," as they were called, would be neatly dressed and well groomed—the "respectable, well-behaved" people the lost laws described.

At all times—even if they were insulted or thrown out onto the street—the checkers were to remain polite. If the black members of the group were served, they were to eat and then leave. If refused service, they were to tell the manager about the anti-discrimination laws of 1872 and 1873. If the manager still wouldn't serve them, they were to leave quietly. In all cases, they were to make a written record of their visit.

The checkers would compile a clearer picture of segregation in Washington restaurants. They would also begin the battle on the second front: convincing restaurants to actually open their doors to black customers.

The first restaurant checks were made on April 8, 1950—eight days after the Municipal Court trial. Between then and the fall of 1950 groups sent out by the Committee made 316 checks in 99 different restaurants. Their survey yielded some surprising results. Of the 316 groups of checkers that visited restaurants, 188 parties were served, and 128 parties were refused service. This amounted to almost 60 percent of the parties being served.

Thirty-eight of the 99 restaurants wouldn't serve the black checkers under any conditions. Twenty-five served them every time without objection, while eight others that at first had refused to serve the black checkers changed their minds following a discussion. Twenty-eight restaurants sometimes did and sometimes didn't serve blacks, often depending on who was on duty as manager.

The bottom line was that 25 percent of the downtown restaurants that were checked served blacks all the time, and more than 60 percent of the establishments were willing to serve blacks at least sometimes.

Previously, blacks had been excluded from all downtown restaurants. What had changed?

Some restaurant owners and managers may have feared that turning away official-looking black people would land them in trouble. Undoubtedly, some knew about the Committee's work and had concluded that since integration was coming, they might as well comply sooner rather than later. Others may have thought about segregation for the first time and decided that it was wrong to exclude people because of their color. And for some, business may have been so slow that they would have served anyone—as long as they paid.

Even in restaurants that refused to serve them, the staff often showed sympathy for the black customers. Some owners and managers confessed that they would gladly change their policy if other restaurants would do so, too, or if the courts ordered them to integrate their establishments. Many waiters and waitresses apologized for refusing service and explained that they had to follow orders. The black waiters and waitresses were particularly upset that, in order to keep their jobs, they couldn't serve members of their own race.

The attitude of the white customers was especially heartening. During the 316 restaurant visits, no white customer complained or in any way seemed annoyed by the presence of black people. In a summary of the restaurant survey issued in October of 1950, the Committee wrote: "The checkers reported that occasionally there was curiosity, but that the usual attitude of the white patrons was one of indifference." In fact, when there were reactions, they were in *favor* of the black customers. For example, white customers sometimes encouraged the black checkers not to give up and even offered to order for them so they wouldn't go hungry.

"It is perfectly clear from this survey," the report concluded, "that Washingtonians are fully ready to welcome a change in present segregation practices in D.C. restaurants and that no disorder will attend such a change."

Pittsburgh Courier *article reporting the first court decision, which went against Mrs. Terrell and the Committee.*

D. C. Cafes Can Refuse Negroes, Court Rules

WASHINGTON—While the United States Government continues to call for fighting men of all races and nations to stem the Communist tide in Korea, Negro citizens in the nation's capital were stunned Tuesday to learn that restaurants here can legally refuse to serve Negro customers.

Walter White, executive secretary of the NAACP, attacked the decision as "deeply disappointing."

Municipal Court Judge Frank H. Myers, ruled that the two "last" anti-discrimination statues of 1872-73 "have both been repealed by implication and cannot legally be enforced."

In his attack on the court, Walter White said: "Judge Myers' decision will have terrible repercussions throughout Asia, Africa, and Latin America, whose colored peoples we are asking to support our action in Korea."

Mr. White said that "Radio Moscow will tell the world in the next twenty-four hours that the Nation's Capital is still jim crow by judicial decision."

TEST CASE

The discouraging ruling was made in a test case on behalf of Dr. Mary Church Terrell, prominent educator and former member of the D. C. School Board. Essie Thompson and Arthur S. Elmer who were refused service at Thompson's restaurant, 725 Fourteenth Street, N.W., "soley because of their race and color."

The District of Columbia filed in an attempted revival and enforcement of part of old municipal regulations which the court has found as a matter of law to have been superceded."

This case was deliberately used as a frontal attempt to get a court decision on segregated eating.

There was no dispute as to the facts of the refusal on last Feb. 28 to serve the Negro customer.

Judge Myers said the sole question before him was: "Were the Legislative Assembly Acts of 1872 and 1873 validly enacted and were these Acts in full force and effect on Feb. 28, 1950?" In his opinion, he answered his own question by ruling that the Supreme Court held—in 1891—that the Organic Act of 1878, an Act long cited by civil right attorneys interested in the elimination of Washington jim crow "was intended to supercede previous laws relating to the same subject matter and to provide a system of government complete in itself in all respects."

ADMITS EATING PROBLEM

"The Court recognizes that it is a real problem in the District of Columbia for members of the

The court decision did not go as well as the restaurant survey. On July 10, 1950, Judge Frank H. Myers ruled that although the lost laws had never been formally repealed, they had been ignored for so long that they had been "repealed by implication" and could not be used to fight Jim Crow.

Many Committee members were shocked and depressed by this defeat. They had been dealt a severe blow, Mary Church Terrell knew, yet she felt that all was not lost and that they were "still in the ring," as she had written to her husband fifty years earlier. Times like these made it clear that she had been a wise choice as chairman.

Annie Stein, the Committee's executive secretary, sent Mrs. Terrell a letter on August 27, 1950, in which she expressed how much the older woman's cheerful confidence meant to her. "I am filled with unbounded admiration for you, dear Mrs. Terrell," wrote Mrs. Stein, "and working with you has been one of the great joys of my life. I will never stop drawing inspiration and courage from your indomitable spirit."

Mary Church Terrell had reason to be hopeful. There were other, higher courts where the outcome might be different.

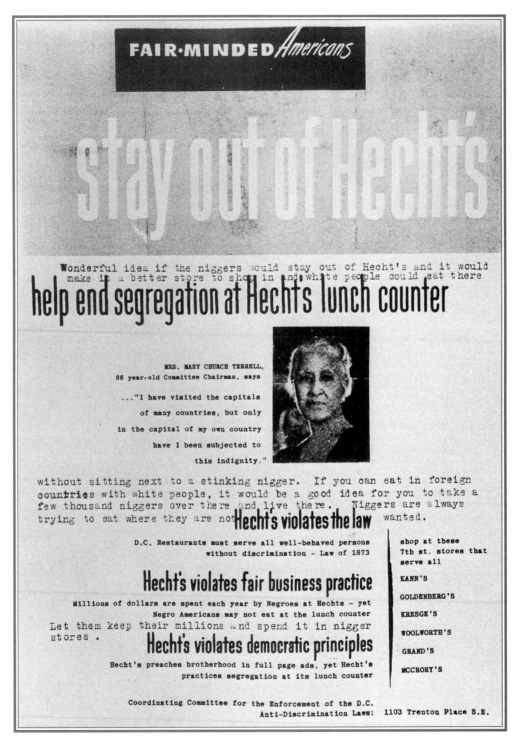

The hate letter that was nailed to Mrs. Terrell's front door; someone typed racist remarks on one of the Committee's flyers.

"Fight On"

Immediately after Judge Myers ruled against it, the Committee began pressing the District's lawyers to take the case to a higher court. A month later attorney Clark King of the corporation counsel's office did so, filing an appeal in the Municipal Court of Appeals on August 7, 1950.

Mary Church Terrell's step-grandson, Raymond L. Langston, remembers her mood at that time. "She took the court cases in stride," recalls Mr. Langston, who was ten years old when Judge Myers made his ruling. "She was a warm and gentle person and everyone liked her, but she could also be tough and persistent. She encouraged the lawyers not to give up—to press on. She thought it was part of the process to continue on, and she trusted her legal team to keep fighting."

Mrs. Terrell's daughters had no children of their own. Phyllis, however, had been married three times. Raymond L. Langston is Phyllis's third husband's son by an earlier marriage. Today, Mr. Langston is the mayor of Highland Beach, Maryland, where he and his wife reside in Mary Church Terrell's former vacation house.

Mr. Langston also remembers that during the restaurant campaign his step-grandmother was sometimes the target of threats. "There were phone calls and hang-ups, and when I went picketing with her on several occasions, a few people drove by in cars and called out names and insults." But only once did he see his step-grandmother extremely disturbed. "She came home and found a hate letter nailed to the door of her house," he recalls. Someone had taken one of the Committee's flyers and written racist remarks on it, such as "Niggers are always trying to eat where they are not wanted."

"She was quite upset, and my dad and Phyllis were quite upset, too," says Mr. Langston. "But I can't remember from anything she said that she ever thought of giving up." Incidents like this made her all the more determined to win the struggle.

The Thompson Restaurant Case was now drawing national attention. Federal Judge J. Waties Waring of South Carolina, speaking in New York City, asked a church audience: "How can the United States face the world and demand justice for minorities of the world when we have racial segregation in our own backyard?"

The year 1950 marked the 150th anniversary of Washington, D.C., as the U.S. capital. Many Americans planned trips to the national capital to celebrate the occasion. In July, Governor Chester Bowles of Connecticut issued a statement in which he urged the people of his state to be aware of the city's shortcomings when they visited the nation's capital.

"I hope you will investigate one aspect of Washington which reflects discredit on all of us," said Governor Bowles. "I am talking about the practice of segregating our Negro citizens in the capital of the United States. Negroes are barred from so-called 'white' restaurants and theaters. They are barred from the big hotels. Their children are forced to go to special Negro schools. Such segregation is accepted practice throughout most of the South. It is defended on the ground that decisions on such matters are solely the business of the various states. But Washington is not the capital of Mississippi or Georgia. Washington is our capital—the capital city of all American people."

Many fair-minded people donated money to the Committee's restaurant campaign. A woman in Miles City, Montana, sent $10. From Liberia, Africa, G. B. Pettengill and his wife sent $28. At her eighty-eighth birthday party Mary Church Terrell raised $113.41 for the Committee. Other individuals and organizations sent donations ranging from a quarter to about $100.

While awaiting the Municipal Court of Appeals decision, Mrs. Terrell

Mary Church Terrell picketing with the Reverend William Jernagin and others; Reverend Jernagin is holding a sign that reads "Ministers of the Gospel Say End Discrimination."

decided to put still more pressure on restaurants that continued to discriminate. Having completed its survey, the Committee made lists of restaurants that did or did not serve black customers. Above the names of the "good" eating places was the advice: "Patronize this growing list of restaurants that serve without discrimination!"

The lists were distributed throughout Washington and sent to newspapers. "List Published of the 36 White-Owned Restaurants in D.C. Serving All Comers," the February 24, 1951, *Washington Afro-American* proclaimed. The article named what it called the "democratic eating places" and stated: "The committee, headed by Mrs. Mary Church Terrell, urged District residents to patronize the dining places that seat and serve ALL without DISCRIMINATION. It also suggested that residents notify the committee if service is refused."

Mrs. Terrell made speeches about the lost laws, often in churches. A number of people who attended meetings where Mrs. Terrell spoke still remember her vividly. William D. Byrd of Washington was one of them. Now a retired federal government worker, Mr. Byrd recalls a phrase Mrs. Terrell used repeatedly about department stores that wouldn't allow blacks to eat at their lunch counters. "She would say, 'Don't shop where you can't eat. Don't shop where you can't eat.'" Mr. Byrd added: "People looked to her for leadership. She never seemed discouraged, never seemed to have doubts, and was always firm for what she wanted to do."

Deep in their hearts—or perhaps in their wallets as their business dwindled—restaurant owners on the "bad" list felt the error of their ways. Gradually, more eating places began serving black customers.

The three judges on the Municipal Court of Appeals issued their ruling on May 24, 1951—nearly a year after Judge Myers had ruled against the Committee. It was a split decision. One judge supported Judge Myers's ruling that the lost laws were dead. A second judge believed the laws were still in force, and the chief judge of the court, Nathan Cayton, agreed. "I believe the 1873 Acts of the Legislative Assembly must stand," Judge Cayton concluded. By a 2–1 vote the Municipal Court of Appeals had ruled that the lost laws could be used to fight discrimination in Washington, D.C.

"Jim Crow Takes Beating" proclaimed the *Washington Afro-American*. Mrs. Terrell was bombarded by phone calls and telegrams. Annie Stein, in New York City at the time, sent her a telegram saying, "Congratulations to our beloved leader on a magnificient victory." Another friend sent a telegram comparing her to Abraham Lincoln and Mahatma Gandhi of India:

CONGRATULATIONS ON YOUR GREAT ACHIEVEMENT AS ANNOUNCED BY THE COURT YESTERDAY. YOU HAVE WON A PLACE BESIDE LINCOLN AND GANDHI THE GREAT EMANCIPATORS BY YOUR COURAGEOUS AND PERSISTENT EFFORTS TO OPEN THE DOOR TO A HAPPIER LIFE FOR A GRATEFUL PEOPLE. MAY YOUR DAYS BE LONG IN THE LAND WHICH YOU HAVE STRIVEN SO HARD TO MAKE MORE BEAUTIFUL FOR ALL OF US. GOD BLESS YOU.

RUTH TRAVERS

Just as she had not been dismayed by the previous year's court defeat, Mrs. Terrell was subdued over the Municipal Court of Appeals victory. Although they had won for the time being, she knew that the struggle was not over. Thompson's Cafeteria and the Washington Restaurant Association would undoubtedly take the case to a still higher court—the United States Court of Appeals for the District of Columbia. That was precisely what they did, which meant that there would be another round in the legal battle.

On June 15, 1951, at a mass meeting of the Committee and its supporters at a Washington church, Mrs. Terrell warned that the fight must continue. At the end of her twenty-minute speech she made one of the most inspiring statements of her career.

"Let us continue to wage a holy war against discrimination and segre-

Pittsburgh Courier article about the second court decision—a victory for Mrs. Terrell and the Committee.

Negroes Win Suit

D. C. Cafe Bias Ruled Illegal

WASHINGTON — By a two-to-one majority vote last Thursday, the Municipal Court of Appeals ruled that an 1873 "lost law" forbidding discrimination by restaurants against "any well-behaved or respectable person" was still legal and valid. It thus declared that any such bias was a violation of D. C. laws.

The decision was made in the case of Dr. Mary Church Terrell, the Rev. Arthur E. Elmes and Miss Jean J. Williams, the latter white, against Thompson's Restaurant which refused to serve Negroes in Feburary, 1950. The trio filed suit on the basis of laws passed in 1872 and 1873 which, for unknown reasons, have not been put on District law books since 1900. Restaurant owners have appealed the decision.
— BUY 1, SELL 2 BTW COINS —

gation and all the other evils which race prejudice forces us to endure!" declared the eighty-seven-year-old leader. "Let us decide right here and now—decide tonight—to allow neither death nor powers nor things present nor things to come to stop us in our efforts to secure all the rights, privileges, and opportunities to which the Constitution of the United States entitles us and which justice demands we should be allowed to enjoy!"

Meanwhile, Mrs. Terrell had stepped up the battle against restaurants that maintained color barriers. First there had been the surveys, followed by the lists of restaurants that did or did not discriminate. Now the Committee targeted several big stores where black people either weren't allowed to eat or were forced to eat standing in separate "Negro sections." The Committee had decided to boycott these stores, which meant convincing people not to shop there until the stores ended their Jim Crow policies.

In late 1950 the Committee had begun a boycott of Kresge's dime store at 7th and E Streets. On the first two days of December, volunteers passed out to shoppers ten thousand leaflets that urged:

DON'T BUY ANYTHING IN KRESGE 7TH & E
KRESGE'S ALLOWS ONLY WHITES TO SIT DOWN AND EAT
KRESGE'S JIM CROW POLICY IS A BLOT ON THE NATION
HELP BRING DEMOCRACY TO THE NATION'S CAPITAL

Expense records show that at about this time the Committee spent $4.64 for "Paints and boards." These were used to create dozens of DON'T BUY AT KRESGE'S signs. Each weekend, volunteers walked back and forth in front of Kresge's, holding up their signs and passing out more leaflets. Mary Church Terrell led the first group of picketers, who paraded in front of Kresge's in a snowstorm. Eventually, more than forty thousand leaflets were distributed and nearly one hundred volunteers took part in picketing Kresge's. Many Christmas shoppers took their business elsewhere when they read the leaflets and saw the picketers in front of the store.

Some Committee members brought their children along to picket. One of the young picketers was Annie Stein's daughter, Eleanor, who was only five years old in 1951. "I walked the picket lines with my mother many times," Eleanor Stein recalls. "At first I was embarrassed to have people staring at me, but after a while I understood the basic point. We were putting pressure on businesses because black people couldn't eat at public establishments in the nation's capital."

Eleanor Stein has many other memories of Mrs. Terrell from the restaurant campaign period. "I met Mary Church Terrell often when I was a very young child. She was elegant, sharp as a tack, dignified, and very purposeful. I think she enjoyed the campaign—both the successes and the fight."

Eleanor also remembers that, busy though Mrs. Terrell was with the

Eighty-seven-year-old Mary Church Terrell picketing Kresge's, as shown in the Washington Afro-American.

restaurant battle, the famous civil rights worker found time for her. "I thought of her as a good friend even though I was five and she was eighty-seven years old. I enjoyed going to her house, where she would serve us treats, and once she took me shopping and bought me a beautiful doll. I felt very close to her. You know how adults can talk down to children? Mrs. Terrell treated me as if I were her equal. She would ask me about school, how my brother was treating me, and talk to me about the campaign."

The campaign was going well in early 1951. On January 12 the Kresge's store manager gave in to the pressure of about six weeks of picketing and assured the Committee that, from then on, no Kresge's store in Washington would bar black people from its sit-down lunch counter.

Next the Committee targeted Hecht's, Washington's largest department store. Hecht's, which had many black shoppers, claimed to believe in equality. On February 19, 1951, Hecht's ran a newspaper ad showing a white hand clasping a black hand. "We can't blind ourselves to the disturbing racial and religious antagonisms in America," proclaimed the ad. "They will defeat our good intentions until we cast them out and live as brothers in our states and neighborhoods—not for a single week, but day by day and year by year. SUPPORT WORLD BROTHERHOOD WEEK FEBRUARY 18–25." But while paying lip service to brotherhood, Hecht's would not allow black customers to sit at its lunch counters.

Mary Church Terrell, Annie Stein, and several other people visited a Hecht's company official. He admitted that the ad had been a publicity gimmick and that the firm didn't plan to integrate its dining areas.

On May 1, 1951, Mrs. Terrell began a boycott against the Hecht's stores on Washington's 7th Street and in nearby Silver Spring, Maryland. This was one of the biggest single civil rights campaigns that had taken place in the United States up to that time. The Committee passed out 100,000 leaflets saying such things as: "Stay out of Hecht's until all are served without discrimination at their lunch counter" and "Hecht's preaches brotherhood, Hecht's practices segregation at its basement lunch counter."

The Committee also distributed "pledge cards" to Hecht's customers. On the front, these postcards were addressed to Hecht's general manager. On the back, customers signed their names to the pledge: "I will not buy at Hecht's until ALL are served without discrimination at the basement lunch counter." Week after week, thousands of pledge cards flooded the Hecht's office.

Hecht's wouldn't change its policy, so in June Mrs. Terrell began weekly "sit-downs" in the 7th Street store. Defying Hecht's rules, black Committee members sat at the store's lunch counter. The management did not serve them but, to avoid a scene, did not call the police, either. Since the "sit-downers" occupied many seats without being served, the lunch counter lost thousands of dollars. This campaign, and a similar one at a Chicago restaurant in 1943, helped inspire the sit-ins of the 1960s. These were protests in which black people defied segregation by refusing to budge from places designated "whites only."

Starting July 20, 1951, Mrs. Terrell sent out large groups to picket Hecht's 7th Street store. Generally composed of about a hundred people, the picket lines marched outside Hecht's three days a week for six months in all kinds of weather. The slogans painted on the picketers' signs discouraged many shoppers from entering Hecht's:

STAY OUT
SEGREGATION PRACTICED HERE

NEGROES SPENT 1/2 MILLION DOLLARS
AT HECHT'S LAST YEAR
YET HECHT'S WON'T SERVE NEGROES
AT ITS LUNCH COUNTER

DON'T BUY AT HECHT'S
HECHT'S JIM CROW LUNCH COUNTER
DISGRACES THE NATION'S CAPITAL

Late in 1951 the Committee members had a brainstorm. Shortly before Christmas the picketers arrived at Hecht's dressed as Santa Claus and other holiday characters. Dozens of people intending to go to Hecht's changed their minds. Who would shop in a store against the advice of

"Stay out of Hecht's" leaflet from around the time of the "Santa Claus picket line."

Santa Claus? Hecht's officials were so furious about the "Santa Claus picket line" that they called the police, but law enforcement officials refused to arrest Santa and his helpers.

By early 1952 the boycott had cost Hecht's six million dollars. The firm had lost thousands of customers. The company decided that it couldn't continue such losses. In mid–January of 1952 Hecht's began serving everyone at its lunch counters.

Mary Church Terrell celebrated by taking a party of black and white people to have lunch at Hecht's. Eating a ham sandwich and a piece of banana custard pie, Mrs. Terrell told reporters that she was "overjoyed" at Hecht's change of policy. "It's a wonderful victory," she said. "I'm happy because it's a victory for justice and equal rights for a minority group. It shows that if we fight we get our rights. I believe that we have to fight."

The Committee used similar tactics at other stores. The "sit-downers" were so patient and polite—and refusing to serve them was so obviously unfair—that more and more white Washingtonians were won over. Some white customers returned everything they had bought to stores that discriminated, or showed displeasure with the stores in other ways.

For example, one day a waitress asked a high-ranking military officer what he wanted at a lunch counter the Committee was trying to integrate. "This other man was here before me," replied the officer, referring to the black sit-downer next to him. "Serve him."

"He can't be served because he's colored," the waitress answered.

Learning that the sit-downer wanted a cola, the officer ordered one for himself. When it came, he set it before the black man. The waitress was annoyed—and even more so when the officer ordered five more colas and set them all in front of the sit-downer. Before leaving, the officer complained to the manager about the store's discriminatory policies.

The Lansburgh department store in downtown Washington integrated its lunch counter in March of 1952 after a six-week campaign by the Committee. That September Murphy's dime store gave in and integrated its lunch counter following a four-month campaign. Shortly before her eighty-ninth birthday, Mrs. Terrell celebrated this victory by having lunch with Annie Stein at Murphy's.

With each fresh triumph, congratulations poured in. "I rejoice with you in the victory over Murphy's," Washington minister Orris G. Robinson of Calvary Methodist Church wrote to Mrs. Terrell. "This is only one of your many victories of the years, but it indicates progress in human relations and the eternal spirit of youth of the chairman, Mary Church Terrell. Fight on, good soldier."

She did fight on, but there were two thousand eating establishments in Washington. Integrating them all by picketing, sit-downs, and discussions could take a century! Besides, unless forced to by law, even those restaurants that had begun to admit blacks might return to their old ways. This was why it was so crucial for the United States Court of Appeals for the District of Columbia to rule in the Committee's favor.

Leaflet from the Murphy's campaign.

The nine judges on this court had heard the case on January 7, 1952. On January 9, 1953, Annie Stein sent Mrs. Terrell a note expressing how eager the Committee was for the judges' ruling. "Our 1st anniversary of the court hearing is over and past and STILL NO DECISION!" wrote Mrs. Stein. "Can we really stand any more waiting?"

The decision came thirteen days later, on January 22, 1953. The Committee members were stunned by what they heard. By a vote of five to four, the judges had ruled that the anti-discrimination laws of 1872 and 1873 "were not valid because of disuse."

"The United States Court of Appeals, dividing 5 to 4, ruled today that eating places in the Capital may refuse service to Negroes," announced the *Los Angeles Examiner.* Newspapers in other cities ran similar stories. To Mrs. Terrell

Cafe Jim Crow In D.C. Upheld

By ALICE DUNNIGAN

WASHINGTON (ANP) — Jim crow has been permitted to "rule the roost" in Washington restaurants by authority of the United States Court of Appeals here.

After more than a year's deliberation on the validity of the "lost laws" of 1872 and 1873, prohibiting segregation in restaurants in the District of Columbia, the court decided, Thursday, by a 5-4 vote, that the old laws are invalid.

The "lost laws" were brought to a test when Mrs. Mary

Pittsburgh Courier article reporting the devastating 5-4 defeat in the U.S. Court of Appeals—the third court decision.

the decision was incredibly unjust. In effect, the judges had said that a community could kill a law by ignoring it long enough.

By this time Mary Church Terrell was eighty-nine years old. The thought must have crossed her mind that she might never get to see a victorious conclusion to the restaurant campaign. Three years had passed since she had entered Thompson's Cafeteria with the Reverend William Jernagin, Mrs. Geneva Brown, and David Scull—three years of meetings, boycotts, sit-downs, picketing, legal work, and waiting. During that time the Committee had lost in the Municipal Court of the District of Columbia, won in the Municipal Court of Appeals, and now—by the razor-thin margin of a single vote—lost in the U.S. Court of Appeals. How much more could she endure?

Her doubts vanished quickly. As shock turned to anger, Mary Church Terrell began planning her strategy for the final round of the battle.

In 1951, students from Washington's Terrell Junior High School (named for her husband) presented Mrs. Terrell with flowers for her 88th birthday; today the U.S. capital also has a Mary Church Terrell Elementary School.

"Your Long and Valiant Struggle"

Mrs. Terrell had prepared two statements in anticipation of the U.S. Court of Appeals decision. She had hoped to use her victory speech. Instead, on January 22, 1953, the day of the decision, she put on a brave face and presented the statement she had prepared in case of defeat:

> *I consider today's majority decision in the Thompson Restaurant Case a tragedy for the United States. The four-fifths of the world's population who are colored people will be shocked by this ruling and by the moral justification given to the evil of segregation by the court.*

Then she proclaimed what the Committee would do next. "The important issue of segregation in the District of Columbia must be carried to the U.S. Supreme Court," she announced. They would take their struggle to the highest court in the country. After that, the battle would be over one way or the other.

Requesting that the U.S. Supreme Court consider a case did not mean that it would automatically do so. The Supreme Court might agree to hear the Thompson Restaurant Case. It could also refuse to do so. The first hurdle was passed when the court decided that this case was important enough for its consideration. The case was scheduled to come before the highest court in the land that spring.

President Dwight D. Eisenhower.

In the weeks before the Supreme Court hearing, Mrs. Terrell, the Committee, and their legal team spent long days plotting strategy. A few months earlier, in November 1952, Dwight D. Eisenhower had been elected president of the United States. During his campaign, Eisenhower had said: "I believe we should eliminate every vestige of segregation in the District of Columbia." This seemed to show that he sided with the Committee. In early 1953 Eisenhower's political party had backed up his words to a tiny degree. Republican officials asked that Washington restaurants and hotels admit black people for a three-day period around the time of Eisenhower's inauguration on January 20, 1953.

Mary Church Terrell knew that the Republicans hadn't done this solely out of the goodness of their hearts. They hoped to avoid the embarrassment of having African American visitors or dark-skinned foreign guests turned away from the city's hotels and restaurants during the inauguration. Mrs. Terrell saw her golden opportunity to point out that discrimination was wrong at *any* time. The Committee printed and distributed thousands of leaflets showing a picture of a black man and a white man nailing down a welcome mat, accompanied by this message:

> HELP NAIL DOWN THE WELCOME MAT IN WASHINGTON D.C.
> DEMOCRACY FOR JUST THREE INAUGURATION DAYS IS *NOT*
> ENOUGH! WE SAY: DEMOCRACY IS A YEAR-ROUND AFFAIR. ALL
> AMERICANS SHOULD BE WELCOME ANYWHERE IN OUR
> NATION'S CAPITAL REGARDLESS OF COLOR. TO ENSURE A
> PERMANENT WELCOME FOR EVERYONE WRITE:
> PRESIDENT DWIGHT D. EISENHOWER
> WHITE HOUSE
> WASHINGTON, D.C.

The Committee also circulated the following petition and then sent signed copies to President Eisenhower and to city officials of Washington:

> WE, THE CITIZENS OF WASHINGTON, D.C., ARE SICK OF
> SEGREGATION. IT IS WRONG AND INDEFENSIBLE. WE, THE
> UNDERSIGNED WHILE AWAITING THE SUPREME COURT
> REVIEW . . . URGE YOU TO TAKE PROMPT ACTION TO FULFILL
> THE PRESIDENT'S PLEDGE TO END ALL SEGREGATION IN THE
> NATION'S CAPITAL.

The leaflets and petitions were a reminder to the nation—including the nine Supreme Court justices—that the president had expressed his determination to end segregation in Washington. Pressuring the president might also achieve something else, Mary Church Terrell hoped. As she wrote in a letter to Committee members, Mrs. Terrell wanted the president to "ask the U.S. Attorney General to intervene in the case before the Supreme Court." Appointed by the president, the attorney general heads the nation's Department of Justice and is the chief law officer of the United States.

The Thompson Restaurant Case came before the Supreme Court on April 30 and May 1, 1953. Justice Robert Jackson was ill, but the remaining eight justices listened to the arguments. Mary Church Terrell, Reverend Jernagin, and several other Committee members were in the courtroom as the lawyers repeated their arguments from the three previous court cases. The legal team for Thompson's Cafeteria and the Washington Restaurant Association again claimed that the lost laws were no longer valid because they had been ignored for so long. The legal team for the Washington commissioners and the Committee again insisted that the old laws were still in effect.

As Mrs. Terrell had hoped, Attorney General Herbert Brownell Jr. had become involved in the case. He sent his special assistant, Philip Elman, to help argue the point that the lost laws remained in force. Mr. Elman repeated what Mary Church Terrell had often said, that segregation in the nation's capital reflected badly on the entire country.

Mary Church Terrell in 1953, before a bust of Frederick Douglass.

Chief Justice Frederick M. Vinson asked Mr. Elman whether the laws of 1872 and 1873 had been repealed in subsequent years. "That is rather important," the chief justice said.

The laws had never been repealed, Mr. Elman responded. The Supreme Court had ruled many times that ignoring laws was not a good reason to throw them out, he added. Coming from the Department of Justice of the United States, Mr. Elman's arguments carried great weight.

At one point Chief Justice Vinson objected to the use of the phrase "lost laws." Although the old laws had been long forgotten, he seemed to feel, the fact that they still existed in a few rare books meant that they had not been completely lost.

The arguments ended on May 1. The justices issued their decision a little over a month later.

On June 8, 1953, Justice William O. Douglas rose and presented the high court's ruling. "The failure to enforce a law does not result in its repeal," he said, expressing the Supreme Court's opinion. Because he had missed the arguments due to illness, Justice Robert Jackson had not voted, but the other justices had decided that the anti–discrimination laws of 1872 and 1873 must be enforced. Their vote was unanimous, 8–0, in favor of ordering all Washington eating places to accept black customers. The eating places were granted only two days to comply with the law.

"I'm so excited that I don't know what to say," Mrs. Terrell told the *Washington Afro-American.* "We have been fighting this case more than three years and have been trying to be hopeful and patient, praying for a favorable decision. It would have been a great tragedy and would have hurt the reputation of this country if the United States Supreme Court had not rendered that decision against the Thompson Restaurant. I hate to think what an adverse decision would have meant especially to our children who have had to grow up feeling inferior to other people."

A Boston woman wrote one of the most eloquent of the congratulatory messages that poured in from around the nation. "We just heard, by radio, the wonderful news of your victory," Cynthia Anthonsen wrote to Mrs. Terrell. "Congratulations to you and to your faithful committee. Your long and valiant struggle has come at last to a victorious conclusion. You have rendered a great service not only to the people of Washington but to the entire country."

But Mrs. Terrell knew that the fight wasn't won unless restaurants obeyed the Supreme Court decision. On June 9, the day after the ruling, she issued a warning on behalf of the Committee. "We warn all eating places that the penalty for violating the law is not only a hundred-dollar fine, but also loss for one year of the license to do business," she said. "We will make it our concern to see that all those who violate the law shall receive that penalty." She concluded with a preview of a new project: "We intend to set up a program in the near future to insure that hotel lodging discrimination comes to an end in Washington."

Triumph! Pittsburgh Courier *article announcing the Supreme Court victory in the fourth and final court decision.*

William D. Byrd recalls hearing Mrs. Terrell speak soon after the great Supreme Court victory. "She told people, 'This is no place to stop—we have to keep going,' because there were other places we needed to desegregate," Mr. Byrd remembered, nearly half a century after he last heard her speak.

By June 10 all two thousand Washington eating places had followed the Supreme Court order and had opened their doors to everyone. With their goal achieved, the Committee did not try to have Thompson's Cafeteria lose its license for a year because of its former policy. In fact, few days after the Supreme Court decision, Mary Church Terrell, the Reverend William Jernagin, Mrs. Geneva Brown, Miss Essie Thompson, and David Scull returned to the cafeteria where they had been denied service in 1950.

This time they were served. When Mrs. Terrell reached the cashier's desk, the restaurant manager took her tray containing soup, cake, and coffee, and carried it to the table for her.

After enjoying a lunch of meat, macaroni, shortcake, and tomato juice, eighty-three-year-old Reverend Jernagin had a simple comment: "The food was good and the treatment was fine."

Dressed for the occasion in a light-blue dress and a red hat, Mrs. Terrell spoke to reporters while slowly eating her soup.

She wanted to savor it, for she had been looking forward to this bowl of soup for three and a half years.

Mary Church Terrell took a short "vacation" in the summer of 1953 to do some writing. *Ebony* magazine hired her to write an article on the person she had once called "the greatest man whom this country has produced." Her article, "I Remember Frederick Douglass," appeared in *Ebony* that October.

The Coordinating Committee for the Enforcement of the D.C. Anti-Discrimination Laws continued its work following the Supreme Court victory. It monitored restaurants to make sure they obeyed the law. And soon Mrs. Terrell led the Committee into its next campaign: desegregating Washington's movie theaters and hotels.

They began by contacting movie theater managers. By this time the

In this 1939 photo, a black man is going into a Mississippi movie theater through the "colored" entrance; a bathroom door with a WHITE MEN ONLY *sign is at left.*

fact that Mrs. Terrell and the Committee had started a new campaign was enough to scare some theater owners. Several movie houses indicated that they were ready to drop their color barriers.

Much as she had with visits to Thompson's Cafeteria in 1950, Mary Church Terrell decided to test a theater's policy. September 23, 1953, was her ninetieth birthday. What better way to celebrate than by going to a movie? Mrs. Terrell invited three fellow Committee members to come along: Reverend Jernagin, eighty-year-old former teacher William D. Nixon, and Mrs. Arline Hays, a woman in her seventies who would be the lone white member of the group.

Mrs. Terrell and her friends went to the Capitol Theater in downtown Washington. Reverend Jernagin, whose very dark skin would make it impossible for him to be mistaken for a white person, bought the tickets. All four people were admitted, and they enjoyed the movie, *The Actress.*

"The theater cashier, doorman, and ushers were wonderful," Reverend Jernagin said after they had seen the film. "We had a wonderful time. I don't know when I've had a better time. In fact, I stayed longer at the show than I'd planned."

The visit to the movie house was reported in the newspapers. Tomlinson Todd, who had discovered the lost laws in the Library of Congress, did a broadcast about the theater visit on his *Americans All* radio show.

"I'm sure our listeners will recall that you and Reverend Jernagin helped get the Thompson Restaurant Case started by a lunchtime visit to that eating place," Mr. Todd said to Mrs. Terrell. "Does your visit to the theaters have any connection with the restaurant campaign?"

"Yes it does," Mary Church Terrell told the radio audience. "This is ancient history now, but you remember how much excitement there was when we first heard about the lost anti-discrimination laws, for you were perhaps the first to rediscover them." After reviewing the restaurant case, she added: "The Coordinating Committee decided that places of public entertainment ought to be next. So that was why we happened to be outside a downtown theater on my birthday."

"What are your future plans?" Tomlinson Todd asked.

"We plan to continue our campaign against segregation in the movie houses until all of them drop their color barriers. We also intend to see that all hotel accommodations in this city are opened without discrimination."

Washington's movie theater managers got the picture. If they didn't admit black people, they might have a Supreme Court case on their hands. Within a couple of weeks virtually all of Washington's movie houses had opened their doors to everyone.

A huge ninetieth birthday party was held for Mary Church Terrell on October 10, 1953, not long after her actual birthday. Her birthday luncheon took place at Washington's Hotel Statler. This alone showed that Washington hotels were removing their color barriers, for only recently had the Statler begun to welcome black guests.

More than seven hundred people attended the luncheon. They included friends, family, college presidents, NAACP officials, members of

Mary Church Terrell at her 90th birthday party.

President Eisenhower's administration, and groups from Maryland, Virginia, Pennsylvania, New Jersey, and New York. Speeches were made praising Mrs. Terrell for a lifetime of civil rights work. The Mary Church Terrell Fund was also launched. Its goal was to raise $50,000 to be used to end all racial discrimination in Washington by the time of Mrs. Terrell's one hundredth birthday in 1963.

Finally, Mary Church Terrell was asked to speak. As usual she was gracious, but she didn't want anyone to think that just because she was ninety her work was finished. She mentioned the restaurant campaign, calling it "the longest and hardest of my career." But she especially wanted to talk about her most recent work—the movie theater campaign. "This afternoon I wish to announce that the Coordinating Committee has received assurances from theater managers in the city that all the movie houses are now admitting well-behaved persons regardless of color," she told the crowd. She called the movie theater victory "the shortest and pleasantest campaign of my career" and "my special ninetieth birthday present."

During the next few months, Mrs. Terrell continued the campaign to desegregate Washington hotels. She closely watched the legal battle to integrate the nation's schools, and often remarked, "I shall be happiest the day our schools are unsegregated." She also continued working on behalf of Rosa Ingram and her two sons, who were still imprisoned. In December of 1953 Mrs. Terrell led a group of sixty prominent women from across the nation to meet with Georgia Governor Herman Talmadge in Atlanta in the hope of winning the Ingrams a pardon. She planned to lead another group to Georgia on May 9, 1954—Mother's Day—to visit Mrs. Ingram in prison and to appeal once more for her freedom.

Mary Church Terrell didn't make that Mother's Day pilgrimage to Georgia, or witness the freeing of the Ingrams five years later in 1959.

Around May 1, 1954, her health failed. Suffering from heart problems and also from cancer, the ninety-year-old civil rights leader had trouble getting out of bed. She rallied briefly. On May 17, 1954, the U.S. Supreme Court ruled in the famous *Brown v. Board of Education* case that racial segregation in the nation's public schools must end. One of the last photographs of

Mrs. Terrell studying the May 1954 school desegregation headline.

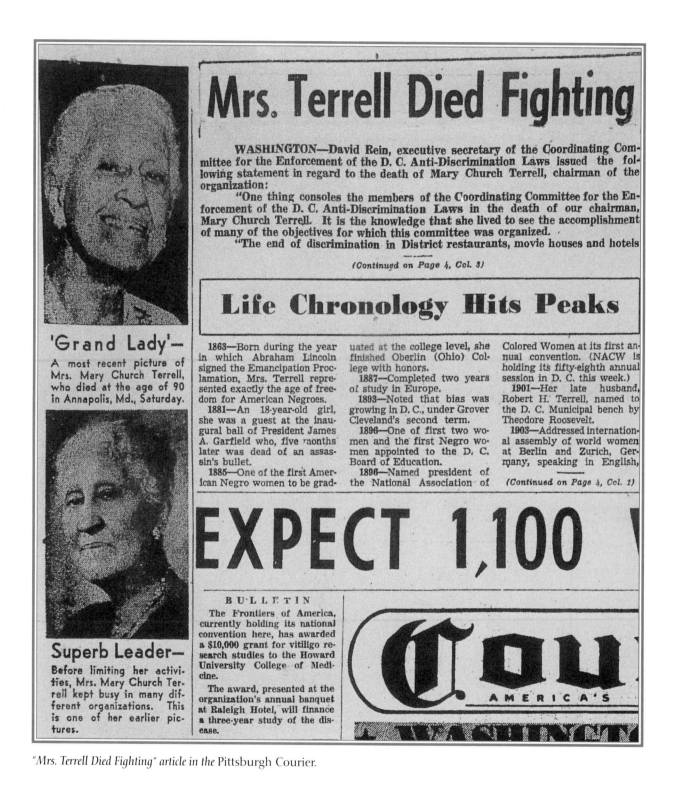

Mrs. Terrell Died Fighting

WASHINGTON—David Rein, executive secretary of the Coordinating Committee for the Enforcement of the D. C. Anti-Discrimination Laws issued the following statement in regard to the death of Mary Church Terrell, chairman of the organization:

"One thing consoles the members of the Coordinating Committee for the Enforcement of the D. C. Anti-Discrimination Laws in the death of our chairman, Mary Church Terrell. It is the knowledge that she lived to see the accomplishment of many of the objectives for which this committee was organized.

"The end of discrimination in District restaurants, movie houses and hotels

(Continued on Page 4, Col. 3)

Life Chronology Hits Peaks

1863—Born during the year in which Abraham Lincoln signed the Emancipation Proclamation, Mrs. Terrell represented exactly the age of freedom for American Negroes.

1881—An 18-year-old girl, she was a guest at the inaugural ball of President James A. Garfield who, five months later was dead of an assassin's bullet.

1885—One of the first American Negro women to be grad-

uated at the college level, she finished Oberlin (Ohio) College with honors.

1887—Completed two years of study in Europe.

1893—Noted that bias was growing in D. C., under Grover Cleveland's second term.

1896—One of first two women and the first Negro women appointed to the D. C. Board of Education.

1896—Named president of the National Association of

Colored Women at its first annual convention. (NACW is holding its fifty-eighth annual session in D. C. this week.)

1901—Her late husband, Robert H. Terrell, named to the D. C. Municipal bench by Theodore Roosevelt.

1903—Addressed international assembly of world women at Berlin and Zurich, Germany, speaking in English,

(Continued on Page 4, Col. 1)

EXPECT 1,100

BULLETIN

The Frontiers of America, currently holding its national convention here, has awarded a $10,000 grant for vitiligo research studies to the Howard University College of Medicine.

The award, presented at the organization's annual banquet at Raleigh Hotel, will finance a three-year study of the disease.

'Grand Lady'—
A most recent picture of Mrs. Mary Church Terrell, who died at the age of 90 in Annapolis, Md., Saturday.

Superb Leader—
Before limiting her activities, Mrs. Mary Church Terrell kept busy in many different organizations. This is one of her earlier pictures.

"Mrs. Terrell Died Fighting" article in the Pittsburgh Courier.

Mary Church Terrell, showing her sitting up and reading about the school integration decision, appeared in the *Washington Afro-American* on June 19, 1954. But Mrs. Terrell's improvement didn't last long.

She spent her last days at her summer home in Highland Beach, Maryland, with her daughter Phyllis caring for her. In late July she was taken to the hospital in Annapolis. She died there on the afternoon of July 24, 1954, two months shy of her ninety-first birthday. Only a few days before her death she had edited some letters the Committee was sending out about a new crusade: ending job discrimination in Washington.

Stirring tributes to Mary Church Terrell were sent to her daughters, Phyllis and Mary. Newspapers ran stories about Mrs. Terrell, reviewing her achievements as the first black woman on Washington's Board of Education, a founder of the NACW and the NAACP, and the leader of the fight to integrate restaurants in the nation's capital.

Famed black educator Mary McLeod Bethune said: "My heart is saddened over the passing of Mary Church Terrell, one of the great women of her time. The services that she rendered humanity will live long after her departure."

Singer and actor Paul Robeson commented: "America loses one of her great daughters, a worthy sister of Frederick Douglass, Harriet Tubman, and Sojourner Truth in her unceasing militant struggle for full citizenship of her people."

Mary Church Terrell would have liked the headline in the *Pittsburgh Courier* best of all. It read:

MRS. TERRELL DIED FIGHTING

A symbolic act: In this photo dating from 1944, marchers in Detroit, Michigan, express the hope that Jim Crow will be dead and buried.

"Those Who Will Follow After You"

Having helped to begin the modern civil rights movement, Mary Church Terrell would have been pleased by much of what occurred in the years after her death. Had she lived a year and a half longer, she would have applauded Rosa Parks for refusing to give up her seat to a white passenger on a bus in Montgomery, Alabama. Had Mrs. Terrell been granted a few more years, she might have marched alongside Dr. Martin Luther King Jr. as he held protests modeled in part after her own anti-segregation drives in Washington. Had she reached her hundredth birthday, as her friends had hoped, she might have joined the giant "March on Washington" in 1963 at which Dr. King made his "I Have a Dream" speech. And had she lived to the ripe old age of 101, Mrs. Terrell would have celebrated the Civil Rights Act of 1964, a national law banning discrimination because of race, sex, religion, or ethnic background.

But if Mary Church Terrell could come back and visit the United States today, she would undoubtedly be disappointed in many ways. Half a century after her death, black Americans still live in segregated neighborhoods in many cities—segregated not by law but by tradition as well as economics. Many African American children attend inner-city schools that aren't nearly as good as they should be. On average, black Americans don't earn as much money, receive as good medical care, or live as long as the rest of the population.

For Mrs. Terrell's ninetieth birthday her friend Mary McLeod Bethune had sent her a letter extending her congratulations. "The work that you have done, the battles that you have fought and won, will forever stand as a monument of your faith, your courage, and your human understanding," wrote Mrs. Bethune. "You have been a valiant leader."

Looking toward the future, Mrs. Bethune predicted, "Your life will stand out as an example to those who will follow after you."

Source Notes

Mary Church Terrell is abbreviated as MCT.

The Mary Church Terrell Papers at the Library of Congress in Washington, D.C., is abbreviated as MCT Papers—LOC.

Mary Church Terrell's autobiography, *A Colored Woman in a White World*, is referred to as "autobiography."

CHAPTER 1: A BOWL OF SOUP
The facts and dialogue in this chapter come from documents in the MCT Papers—LOC. Of special help were MCT's April 6, 1954, description of what occurred when she and her friends went to Thompson's Cafeteria and the sworn statements of MCT, the Reverend William Jernagin, David Scull, and Mrs. Geneva Brown.

CHAPTER 2: BOB CHURCH'S DAUGHTER
The facts about MCT's early life in this chapter come from her autobiography. The information about MCT's father comes from *Robert Church* by Cookie Lommel and *The Robert R. Churches of Memphis* by Annette E. and Roberta Church.
p. 9 The quote about MCT possibly beginning life "in slavery" is from *Robert Church* by Cookie Lommel, p. 141.

CHAPTER 3: "HOLD HIGH THE BANNER OF MY RACE"
MCT's autobiography provides most of the information for this chapter.
p. 21 The quote about MCT realizing that she was "descended from slaves" is from the autobiography, pp. 20–21.
p. 23 The quote about MCT seeing her name in *St. Nicholas* comes from the autobiography, p. 221.
pp. 24–25 MCT's childhood journal entry "A Moonlight Excursion" is from the MCT Papers—LOC.
pp. 25–26 Much of the information about Memphis and the yellow fever epidemics is from *The Biography of a River Town* by Gerald M. Capers, pp. 194–99.
pp. 26-27 The story of MCT's father buying the first bond for $1,000 appears on p. 115 of *Robert Church* by Cookie Lommel.

CHAPTER 4: "I AM A COLORED GIRL"
Most of the information for this chapter comes from the autobiography. Oberlin College provided the dates of MCT's attendance there.
pp. 35–37 The quote from "The Poor in Our Cities" and information about MCT's other youthful writings come from the MCT Papers—LOC.
p. 37 Information about Robert Church's mansion in Memphis comes from pp. 194–95 of *Robert Church* by Cookie Lommel, and from pp. 33–34 of *The Robert R. Churches of Memphis* by Annette E. and Roberta Church.

CHAPTER 5: "THE WELFARE OF MY RACE"
Most of the incidents in this chapter are based on MCT's accounts in her autobiography.
pp. 44–45 Information about Robert Terrell's early life comes from the MCT Papers—LOC.

p. 50 The quote starting "It's my country" comes from p. 99 of the autobiography.

p. 51 Marietta College provided the date of Thomas Church's graduation.

CHAPTER 6: MR. TERRELL "GOES TO CHURCH"

The MCT Papers—LOC and the autobiography provided the bulk of the material for this chapter.

pp. 53–54 Robert Terrell's letter to Mollie's father and the wedding invitation both come from the MCT Papers—LOC.

pp. 56–57 The information about the black women's clubs comes mainly from *Quest for Equality* by Beverly Washington Jones, pp. 18–19.

pp. 57–58 The visit with President Benjamin Harrison is recounted in MCT's article "I Remember Frederick Douglass" in the October 1953 *Ebony* magazine, pp. 73–80.

p. 58 The letter from Charles W. Chesnutt to MCT is in the MCT Papers—LOC.

CHAPTER 7: "LIFTING AS WE CLIMB"

The MCT Papers—LOC and the autobiography are the main sources for this chapter.

pp. 61–62, 64–65 MCT's article "The Duty of the NACW to the Race" appears in the January 1900 *AME Church Review*, pp. 340–54.

pp. 62–64 MCT's first presidential address to the NACW, as well as the fundraising letter, are from the MCT Papers—LOC.

pp. 67–68 The date of Phyllis's birth and the approximate date that MCT adopted her brother Thomas's daughter, Mary, were provided by Raymond L. Langston, stepson of Phyllis and step-grandson of MCT.

p. 70 Advertisements for MCT's lectures come from the MCT Papers—LOC.

pp. 71–72 The diary entries regarding MCT's travels come from the MCT Papers—LOC.

pp. 72–73 The information about the various Jim Crow laws comes from *The Strange Career of Jim Crow* by C. Vann Woodward.

pp. 73–75 The Texarkana, Arkansas, incident is described on pp. 299–302 of the autobiography, and the Dover, Delaware, incident on pp. 311–15 of the same book.

CHAPTER 8: "I HAVE DONE SO LITTLE"

The letters and diary entries in this chapter come from the MCT Papers—LOC.

pp. 83–84 MCT's comments about wanting to succeed as a story writer appear in her article "Needed: Women Lawyers" in the September 1943 *Negro Digest*, pp. 57–59.

p. 85 MCT's comments about dancing at seventy are from p. 407 of her autobiography.

pp. 86–87 The mountain-climbing incident at Harpers Ferry, West Virginia, is described on pp. 240–42 of the autobiography.

CHAPTER 9: A "MEDDLER"

The information for this chapter comes mostly from MCT's autobiography and from the MCT Papers—LOC.

p. 89 "The Mission of Meddlers" by MCT appears on pp. 566–68 of the August 1905 *Voice of the Negro*.

pp. 90–92 MCT discusses the Brownsville Riot on pp. 268–78 of her autobiography; the event is described in depth in *The Brownsville Affair* by Ann J. Lane.

p. 93 Booker T. Washington's letter to Robert Terrell, written in 1909, appears on p. 44 of *Quest for Equality* by Beverly Washington Jones.

p. 95 "The Justice of Woman Suffrage" is on pp. 243–45 of *The Crisis* of September 1912.

pp. 98–99 MCT's May 18, 1919, letter written in Zurich to her husband comes from the MCT Papers—LOC.

CHAPTER 10: "I INTEND NEVER TO GROW OLD"
Material for this chapter comes primarily from the MCT Papers—LOC, the Mary Church Terrell Papers at the Moorland–Spingarn Research Center at Howard University in Washington, D.C., and the autobiography.

p. 101 Groups MCT belonged to are mentioned in the MCT Papers—LOC.

p. 101 Robert Terrell's involvement with the Capital Savings Bank and his loans from his father-in-law, Robert Church, are mentioned in the Robert R. Church Family Papers, Mississippi Valley Collection, University of Memphis.

pp. 102–105 Information regarding Robert Church's will and later complications come from the Robert R. Church Family Papers.

pp. 102–103 Information about Robert Church's slave wife, Margaret Pico, and their daughter, Laura Church Napier, comes from the November 16, 1928, *Memphis Commercial Appeal*.

pp. 105–106 Details regarding MCT's government jobs are described in the autobiography, pp. 250–59 and 318–28.

pp. 107–11 Information and diary entries about MCT's autobiography come from the MCT Papers—LOC.

p. 111 MCT's quote about intending "never to grow old" comes from p. 407 of her autobiography.

p. 112 The letter from Thomas Church Jr. to MCT comes from the MCT Papers—LOC.

pp. 112–14 Information about MCT's argument with her half-brother, Robert, and her adoption of Thomas Jr. comes from the Mary Church Terrell Papers at the Moorland–Spingarn Research Center at Howard University.

p. 115 The letter to Phyllis saying "Surely you must be ill!" was written by MCT on July 20, 1937, and is in the MCT Papers—LOC.

p. 115 MCT's letter to Phyllis asking about Thomas and explaining how to send an air-mail letter was written on August 6, 1952, and is from the MCT Papers—LOC.

pp. 116–17 The information about MCT's passport, false teeth, auto accident, and fall come from material in the MCT Papers—LOC.

CHAPTER 11: "YOUR INDOMITABLE SPIRIT"
Most of the information about MCT in this chapter is from the MCT Papers—LOC.

p. 119 The letter in which MCT is informed that her membership for the American Association of University Women was rejected is dated October 10, 1946, and is in the MCT Papers—LOC.

p. 120 Material on the Ingrams and MCT's interests in oppressed people of the world is in the MCT Papers—LOC.

pp. 120–22 The quote starting "With very few exceptions" and telling about discrimination against blacks is from p. 89 of *To Secure These Rights* by the President's Committee on Civil Rights.

p. 122 The information about "Negro jobs" is from p. 55 of *Segregation in Washington* by Kenesaw M. Landis.

p. 122 The quote from the Washington Real Estate Board Code of Ethics is from p. 30 of *Segregation in Washington*.

p. 122 The information about death rates among black infants and mothers is from p. 49 of *Segregation in Washington.*

p. 122 The information about overcrowded black schools is from p. 76 of *Segregation in Washington.*

p. 122 The information about colleges that did or didn't discriminate is from p. 78 of *Segregation in Washington.*

pp. 122–23 The Bill of Rights public speaking contest story is told on p. 75 of *Segregation in Washington.*

p. 123 The segregated marbles competition story is related on pp. 140–41 of *To Secure These Rights.*

p. 123 The dog cemetery story is told on p. 19 of *Segregation in Washington.*

p. 123 The description of blacks being turned away from the movie *Home of the Brave* is told in Howard Whitman's article "Washington—Disgrace to the Nation" in the February 1950 *Woman's Home Companion,* pp. 34–48.

pp. 123–24 The story about the Boy Scout gathering in Washington, D.C., comes from the MCT Papers—LOC.

pp. 124–25 The story of Tomlinson Todd talking to MCT about the lost laws is told on pp. 39–40 of *Mary Church Terrell—Respectable Person* by Gladys Byram Shepperd.

pp. 124–25 The lost laws are mentioned on p. 18 of *Segregation in Washington.*

pp. 126–28 The wording of the lost laws is given in various places in the MCT Papers—LOC.

p. 130 Statistics on numbers of members, organizations, and churches in the CCEAD come from p. 52 of *Mary Church Terrell—Respectable Person.*

pp. 132–33 The Washington Restaurant Association letter of March 13, 1950, was printed in the April 1, 1950, *Pittsburgh Courier.*

p. 133 Mrs. Terrell's statement beginning "Those who are trying to enforce the anti-discrimination laws" appears in the MCT Papers—LOC.

pp. 134–36 The statistics, details, and summary of the restaurant checks come from the MCT Papers—LOC.

p. 137 The August 27, 1950, Annie Stein letter to MCT comes from the MCT Papers—LOC.

CHAPTER 12: "FIGHT ON"
The information for this chapter comes primarily from interviews with people who knew MCT and from the MCT Papers—LOC.

pp. 139–40 The authors interviewed Raymond L. Langston about his step-grandmother MCT in September 2001.

p. 140 Governor Chester Bowles's comments were reported in newspapers, including the *Chicago Defender,* in July 1950.

pp. 142 The authors interviewed William D. Byrd in September 2001.

p. 142 The Ruth Travers telegram is in the MCT Papers—LOC.

pp. 143–44 Mrs. Terrell's June 15, 1951, speech is in the MCT Papers—LOC.

pp. 144–46 The authors interviewed Eleanor Stein in September 2001.

pp. 147–48 The "Santa Claus picket line" is described on p. 69 of *Mary Church Terrell—Respectable Person.*

pp. 148–49 MCT's comments about a "victory for justice" were reported in the January 19, 1952, *Washington Afro-American.*

p. 149 The story about the military officer and the sit-downer is told on p. 80 of *Quest for Equality*.

p. 149 The "Fight on" letter is quoted on p. 77 of *Mary Church Terrell—Respectable Person*.

p. 150 The January 9, 1953, note from Annie Stein to MCT is in the MCT Papers—LOC.

CHAPTER 13: "YOUR LONG AND VALIANT STRUGGLE"
Most of the material for this chapter is from the MCT Papers—LOC.

p. 153 MCT's January 22, 1953, statement is from the MCT Papers—LOC.

pp. 157–58 The Cynthia Anthonsen letter was written on June 8, 1953, and is in the MCT Papers—LOC.

p. 158 MCT's June 9, 1953, warning to eating places to obey the law is in the MCT Papers—LOC.

p. 159 William D. Byrd told the authors about MCT's reaction to the Supreme Court victory in September 2001.

p. 159 The visit to Thompson's Cafeteria by MCT, the Reverend William Jernagin, Mrs. Geneva Brown, Miss Essie Thompson, and David Scull is described in the June 20, 1953, *Washington Afro-American*.

pp. 159–61 Information about the movie theater visit is contained in a transcript of Tomlinson Todd's radio show and in newspaper articles in the MCT Papers—LOC.

pp. 161–62 MCT's ninetieth birthday party is described in the MCT Papers—LOC.

p. 165 The remarks about MCT by Mary McLeod Bethune and Paul Robeson appeared in the July 31, 1954, *Washington Afro-American*.

p. 165 The "MRS. TERRELL DIED FIGHTING" headline appeared in the July 31, 1954, *Pittsburgh Courier*.

AFTERWORD: "THOSE WHO WILL FOLLOW AFTER YOU"
p. 167 The ninetieth-birthday letter to MCT from Mary McLeod Bethune was written on October 7, 1953, and comes from the MCT Papers—LOC.

Bibliography

COLLECTIONS OF DOCUMENTS

Mary Church Terrell Papers, Library of Congress, Washington, D.C.

Mary Church Terrell Papers, Moorland–Spingarn Research Center, Howard University, Washington, D.C.

Robert R. Church Family Papers, Mississippi Valley Collection, University of Memphis.

BOOKS

Capers, Gerald M. *The Biography of a River Town*. Chapel Hill, N.C.: University of North Carolina Press, 1939.

Church, Annette E., and Roberta Church. *The Robert R. Churches of Memphis: A Father and Son Who Achieved in Spite of Race*. Ann Arbor: Edwards Brothers, 1974.

Davis, Elizabeth Lindsay. *Lifting as They Climb*. New York: G. K. Hall, 1996 (reprint of 1933 edition).

Jones, Beverly Washington. *Quest for Equality: The Life and Writings of Mary Eliza Church Terrell, 1863–1954*. Brooklyn, N.Y.: Carlson, 1990.

Lamon, Lester C. *Blacks in Tennessee: 1791–1970*. Knoxville: University of Tennessee Press, 1981.

Landis, Kenesaw M. *Segregation in Washington*. Chicago: National Committee on Segregation in the Nation's Capital, 1948.

Lane, Ann J. *The Brownsville Affair: National Crisis and Black Reaction*. Port Washington, N.Y.: Kennikat Press, 1971.

Lommel, Cookie. *Robert Church*. Los Angeles: Melrose Square, 1995.

McIlwaine, Shields. *Memphis Down in Dixie*. New York: E. P. Dutton, 1948.

Palmer, Pamela, editor. *The Robert R. Church Family of Memphis: Guide to the Papers*. Memphis: Memphis State University Press, 1979.

President's Committee on Civil Rights. *To Secure These Rights*. Washington: U.S. Government Printing Office, 1947.

Shepperd, Gladys Byram. *Mary Church Terrell—Respectable Person*. Baltimore: Human Relations Press, 1959.

Sterling, Dorothy. *Black Foremothers: Three Lives*, 2nd ed. New York: Feminist Press, 1988.

Terrell, Mary Church. *A Colored Woman in a White World*. New York: G. K. Hall, 1996 (reprint of 1940 Ransdell edition).

Woodward, C. Vann. *The Strange Career of Jim Crow*, 2nd rev. ed. New York: Oxford University Press, 1966.

ARTICLES

Terrell, Mary Church. "The Disbanding of the Colored Soldiers." *Voice of the Negro*, December 1906, pp. 554–58.

———. "The Duty of the NACW to the Race." *AME Church Review*, January 1900, pp. 340–54.

———. "I Remember Frederick Douglass." *Ebony*, October 1953, pp. 73–80.

———. "The Justice of Woman Suffrage." *The Crisis*, September 1912, pp. 243–45.

———. "The Mission of Meddlers." *Voice of the Negro*, August 1905, pp. 566–68.

———. "Needed: Women Lawyers." *Negro Digest*, September 1943, pp. 57–59.

Whitman, Howard. "Washington—Disgrace to the Nation." *Woman's Home Companion*, February 1950, pp. 34–48.

INTERVIEWS BY THE AUTHORS
(All took place in September 2001)
Mr. William D. Byrd (acquaintance of MCT) and his wife, Mrs. Ann Byrd.
Mr. Raymond L. Langston (step-grandson of MCT) and his wife, Mrs. Jean Langston.
Ms. Eleanor Stein (friend of MCT).

Picture Credits

The photographs in this book are from the following sources and are used by permission and through the courtesy of the copyright owners:

Judith Bloom Fradin: pp. 20, 63, 110

Hon. Raymond and Mrs. Jean Langston, Terrell/Langston Collection; rephotographed by Judith Bloom Fradin: pp. 85, 114, 138

Library of Congress: pp. 2, 6, 8, 32, 34, 35, 40, 43, 44, 45, 49, 56, 57, 60, 62, 66, 69, 72, 74, 76, 83, 88, 92, 93, 94, 96, 97, 104, 108, 121, 124, 125, 148, 150, 154, 160, 167

Memphis/Shelby County Public Library & Information Center: p. 18

Moorland–Spingarn Research Center: pp. 11, 12, 14, 31, 36, 42, 47, 58, 65, 67, 79

National Portrait Gallery, Smithsonian Institution: pp. viii, 118

Oberlin College Archives, Oberlin, Ohio: p. 28

Pittsburgh Courier; rephotographed by Judith Bloom Fradin: pp. 131, 136, 143, 151, 158, 164

St. Nicholas; rephotographed by Judith Bloom Fradin: p. 24

Segregation in Washington; rephotographed by Judith Bloom Fradin: pp. 126, 127

Alonzo N. Smith; rephotographed by Judith Bloom Fradin: p. 86

Eleanor Stein: pp. x, 129, 156

University of Memphis libraries, Church Family Collection, Special Collections Department: pp. 38, 52, 100

Washington Afro-American: pp. 145, 152, 162, 163

Copyright *Washington Post*; reprinted by permission of the Washington, D.C., Public Library: p. 4

Index

Note: Page numbers in **bold** type refer to illustrations